Listening Effectively

Achieving High Standards in Communication

JOHN A. KLINE

Troy State University, Alabama

Prentice Hall

Upper Saddle River, New Jersey
Columbus, Ohio

Library of Congress Cataloging-in-Publication Data

Kline, John A.
   Listening Effectively : achieving high standards in communication / John A. Kline.
      p. cm.
   Includes bibliographical references and index.
   ISBN 0-13-048841-0
    1. Listening. 2. Attention. 3. Interpersonal communication. I. Title

BF323.L5 K548 2003
153.6'8—dc21

2002030346

Vice President and Publisher: Jeffery W. Johnston
Senior Acquisitions Editor: Sande Johnson
Assistant Editor: Cecilia Johnson
Production Editor: Holcomb Hathaway
Design Coordinator: Diane C. Lorenzo
Cover Designer: Jeff Vanik
Cover Art: Illustration Works
Production Manager: Pamela D. Bennett
Director of Marketing: Ann Castel Davis
Director of Advertising: Kevin Flanagan
Marketing Manager: Christina Quadhamer

This book was set in Goudy by The Clarinda Company. It was printed and bound by Banta Book Group. The cover was printed by Phoenix Color Corp.

Pearson Education Ltd.
Pearson Education Australia Pty. Limited
Pearson Education Singapore Pte. Ltd.
Pearson Education North Asia Ltd.
Pearson Education Canada, Ltd.
Pearson Educación de Mexico, S.A. de C.V.
Pearson Education—Japan
Pearson Education Malaysia Pte. Ltd.
Pearson Education, *Upper Saddle River, New Jersey*

Prentice
Hall

10 9 8 7 6 5 4 3 2 1
ISBN 0-13-048841-0

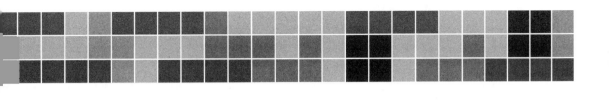

Contents

Types of Listening   43

Instructions for Listening   55

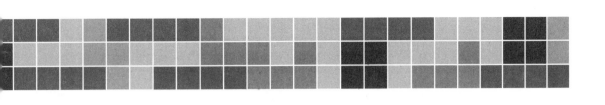

Preface

Most books on listening are too long. They generally contain such material as a detailed discussion of the mechanics of hearing, a lengthy discussion of the process of listening, and chapters devoted to each type of listening. All this information is nice to know but is not necessary if one's goal is simply to become a better listener. Furthermore, although many of these books cover a large amount of material, they surprisingly neglect to give much concrete advice on how to improve listening behavior.

Other books on listening are short, but most of them are lightweight. They don't present theoretically based and acknowledged techniques for improved listening. In other words, they don't tell the reader how to be a better listener. I have made this book substantial enough to cover the subject but brief enough to keep the reader's interest.

The material in this book comes from three decades of study, research, and teaching thousands of people from college students to corporate leaders. For over two decades I taught courses at the United States Air Force's Air University near Montgomery, Alabama. I taught at all levels, from young enlisted personnel to senior officers attending the Air War College. The information in this book is based on material taught to thousands of officers, enlisted personnel, and Air Force civilian employees. It has been taught and, I think, stands the test of time.

ORGANIZATION

The book begins with a chapter that makes a strong case for better listening in all areas of life—in school, at work, and with family and friends. Chapter 2 presents six faulty assumptions people often make that keep them from reaching their potential as listeners. Chapter 3 focuses on nine common bad habits that hinder listening.

Chapter 4 presents the process of listening—receiving, attending, understanding, responding, and remembering. Special emphasis is given to selective listening, barriers to understanding, and memory techniques. Chapter 5 discusses the five types of listening: informative, relational, appreciative, critical, and discriminative.

The sixth and final chapter presents 18 practical instructions for listening drawn from each of the three "domains of learning"—cognitive or thinking, affective or feeling, and psychomotor or doing.

SPECIAL FEATURES

Several features of this book make it particularly attractive both to teachers/trainers and to students/trainees.

Writing Style.   The book is lively and easy to read. Technical jargon is not used. No previous study of the subject is presumed. Many examples and quotations are scattered throughout the book to hold the reader's attention and to support points being made.

Activities.   Some activities are suited for in-class completion. Others are best done in pairs or even by entire classes or training groups. Tests to check listening skills appear at various places in the book.

Helpful Suggestions.   I provide useful suggestions and hints, including techniques to assess a speaker's logical and emotional appeals, improve memory, and stay focused.

ACKNOWLEDGMENTS

Many people have helped me along the way. My sincere thanks to Carol Horton, Regional Editorial Consultant for Prentice Hall, who urged me to write this book; Sande Johnson, Senior Acquisitions Editor at Prentice Hall, who provided encouragement and advice; and Assistant Editor Cecilia Johnson, who was a delight to work with. I would also like to thank Gay Pauley and Karen Swartz, who helped fine-tune the manuscript during copyediting and production.

A special thank you goes to Dr. Richard Cornell, formerly professor and chairman of the Speech Department and director of the Speech and Hearing Clinic of Auburn University at Montgomery; and Dr. Jim Vickrey, professor and chairman of the Department of Speech Communication at Troy State University, who provided helpful suggestions for the final manuscript. Colonel James C. Poole, USAF (ret.), former dean of the Air War College; Dr. James D.

Young, professor emeritus, Troy State University; Helen Henry; and Helene Mooty encouraged my work.

I owe special thanks to my former Ph. D. dissertation advisees, some of whom have been after me for some time to write this book. None of them deserves more thanks than my former student and advisee Dr. Steve Beebe, chair of the Department of Speech Communication and Theatre at Southwest Texas State University. Steve has far surpassed me in both quantity and substance with his many outstanding books in the field of communication. He is an inspiration to me.

The following reviewers made many helpful suggestions, for which I am also grateful: Brent Bass, Le Tourneau University; G. Maxine Beatty, Thomas Nelson Community College; Andrea Berta, The University of Texas at El Paso; John Koscelny, Coffeyville Community College; Ron Lennon, Barry University; and Dona Orr, Boise State University.

Many other mentors, role models, and friends provided encouragement. Dr. Sam Becker, my own Ph. D. dissertation advisor at the University of Iowa over three decades ago, is still my hero. My former boss and friend, General Lance Lord, urged me to write a book on listening. My current boss and colleague, Dr. Jack Hawkins, Jr., chancellor of the Troy State University System, has been unusually supportive. The sermons of my minister and friend, Dr. John Ed Mathison, have taught me that good speakers can make listening easy.

Finally, my wife, Ann, made suggestions and encouraged me throughout the writing process. She has taught me much about how to be a good listener and deserves special thanks.

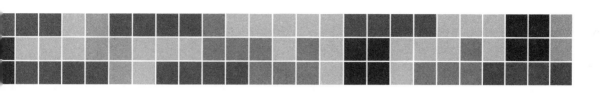

About the Author

John Kline grew up in Iowa, graduated from Iowa State University with a B.A. in English and speech, received his Ph.D. degree in communication from the University of Iowa, and taught at the Universities of New Mexico and Missouri–Columbia before going to the USAF Air University as a civilian professor, where he gained a reputation as the Air Force's leading expert on communication and listening—teaching thousands of officers, as well as enlisted and civilian personnel, how to communicate and listen effectively.

Dr. Kline is now a professor at Troy State University in Alabama. In addition, the Air Force, Army, and large companies regularly call on Dr. Kline to teach their personnel how to communicate more effectively.

Dr. Kline and his wife, Ann, who live in Montgomery, Alabama, have five grown children and twelve grandchildren.

Visit Dr. Kline's website: www.klinespeak.com

Introduction

Why You Should Read This Book

When I am about to read a book, I want to know why I should read it. What can I expect to gain from it? I suspect that you are no different. As a reader, you have a right to know why you should read a book and how you will benefit from it. I'll keep it simple. As you read this book, six things will happen. You will

- know that listening is a key ingredient for success
- learn about six fallacies (mistaken ideas) that keep you from being a good listener
- comprehend and learn how to eliminate nine bad listening habits
- analyze the parts of the listening process and the five types of listening so that you will be a more effective listener
- analyze types of listening so that you will be able to apply the instructions you learn to each type
- learn how to be a better listener in all situations

I hope you agree that these are pretty good reasons for reading this book.

> *The most basic of all human needs is the need to understand and be understood. The best way to understand people is to listen to them.*
>
> Ralph Nichols

INSIGHT

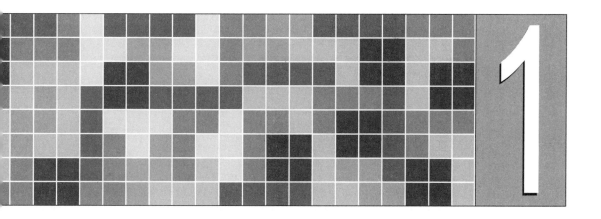

The Need for Better Listening

Objective: Know that listening is a key ingredient for success.

Tasks: Tell how much communication time is devoted to listening.

Give examples of problems resulting from poor listening

Listening is the neglected communication skill. All of us have had instruction in reading, writing, and speaking, but few have had any formal instruction in listening. This void in our education and training is especially interesting in light of research showing that most of us spend nearly 50 minutes of every waking hour in some form of communication. Of these 50 minutes, 15 minutes are spent reading or writing, 10 minutes talking, and 25 minutes listening.

Think of it—we spend half of our communication time listening, but few people make a concerted effort to be better listeners. For those who do, however, the effort pays great dividends: higher productivity, faster learning, better jobs, more promotions, and improved relationships. In some cases, listening determines our physical well-being—perhaps even whether we live or die.

> Each hour we are awake we spend 50 minutes communicating:
> - 15 minutes reading or writing
> - 10 minutes talking
> - 25 minutes listening

WHEN LISTENING IS CRUCIAL

In some jobs good listening is not only important; it is absolutely crucial. Consider the following transcript of a taped conversation between a military pilot and the control tower during routine landing preparations. The tower operator wants the aircraft to descend from 15,000 feet to 8,000 feet and maintain a heading of 180 degrees. Here is the conversation:

Control Tower Operator: "Turn right; keep your heading of 180 degrees. Descend and maintain 8,000 feet."

Pilot: "Right. Maintaining heading of 180 degrees. Am leaving 15,000 and heading for 2,000." *[Notice that both the control tower operator and the pilot were guilty of poor listening. The tower operator told the pilot to maintain 8,000 feet; the pilot said that he was heading for 2,000 feet. Neither of them caught the discrepancy.]*

Pilot: About a minute later the pilot says, "Steady at 180 degrees and am passing 10,000 for 2,000."

Control Tower Operator: "Roger. Your position is 12 miles southwest of airport; maintain 8,000 feet." *[Again there is poor listening. When the tower operator says, "Roger," he is letting the pilot know that he understands and approves of the pilot leaving an altitude of 10,000 feet and descending to 2,000 feet. Then, curiously, the tower operator goes on to restate that the pilot is to maintain an altitude of 8,000 feet.]*

Pilot: "Roger, passing nine for two." *[Here the pilot again demonstrates that he did not listen when the tower operator told him to maintain an altitude of 8,000 feet, for he declares that he is passing 9,000 feet and descending to an altitude of 2,000 feet.]*

Control Tower Operator: Nearly two minutes later the tower operator says: "Your position is 19 miles southwest of airport. Turn right 200 degrees for a slight pattern extension."

The report goes on to say that at this point radar and radio contact were lost. Both the pilot and his copilot crashed into the side of a mountain and died, "victims in a fatal accident, the result of poor listening in the air and on the ground."*

You may not have a job where routine listening has life or death consequences. But the fact is that each of us is placed daily in situations where poor listening threatens our safety. If you drive an automobile, walk across a busy street, work around machinery, or do countless other things in our industrial and technological society, poor listening can put you at risk. That aside, if poor listening keeps you from doing your job well, getting the promotion you deserve, or maintaining good relationships with others, it is well worth the effort to become better at it.

Poor listening is costly in even the most routine staff communications and office operations. Directives to a staff or instructions to office personnel are often given only once—typically orally. The greater the difference in rank or position between those giving the directives or instructions and those receiving them, the less inclined the receivers are to ask for clarification, lest they be considered dull, slow, or inattentive. It is important to listen carefully the first time, and, as discussed later, to ask questions or provide other feedback to make it clear that you are listening.

HOW WELL DO YOU LISTEN?

On the next two pages are two messages. Before you turn to these pages, pair off with another person if you are reading this book in a classroom or training context. If you are reading this book on your own, find someone who will help you—perhaps your spouse, coworker, or friend. One of you can read the first message aloud and ask the questions that follow. Change roles for the second message. In each case, read the message only once. See how well each of you listened by how many questions you can answer correctly. *Note: As a variation on this exercise, choose one person to read the messages to the rest of a group or class.*

---

*"Hearing but Not Listening," USAF *Aerospace Safety*, January 1971, p. 8.

Exercise   Message One: Check Your Listening

Instructions: Read this message aloud to someone one time.

A boss in his mid-fifties calls his employees together and tells them, "I have some important information for you. I want you to listen very carefully, because I plan on making some big changes."

The workers find it difficult to focus on what the boss is about to say. They have all been putting in a lot of overtime and they are tired. Furthermore, the company has been doing well, so they don't understand why any big changes are needed. Also, the boss's personal appearance doesn't make listening any easier. His clothes are a radical departure from his usual apparel. Instead of a dark suit, white shirt, and conservative tie, he is wearing a bright-yellow shirt open at the neck, no jacket, and no socks. His trousers and shoes look like those worn by the young male models in *Gentlemen's Quarterly* or *Esquire*.

The boss continues, apparently unaware that his workers are having problems listening to him. "First," he says, "we are no longer going to sell to the Acme Company. I know that they have been our number-one customer, but I don't agree with their method of doing business—they are just too stodgy and traditional. Second, I am hiring my secretary's brother to be vice-president of all overseas sales. I know that my secretary is young and has only been with me a short time, but she is 'unbelievable' and her brother—well he is from the same genetic pool, so I know he will do a good job. Finally," he concludes, "we are going to change our image to come across as a more youth-oriented and 'with it' company."

Now have the listener(s) answer these questions:

1. What were the three reasons employees had difficulty listening to what the boss had to say?
2. What were the three changes the boss planned to make?
3. What was the boss wearing?
4. Can you "read between the lines"—can you see what may have caused the boss to want to make these changes? Give your assessment.

Now ask the listener(s) to determine why they could answer some questions better than others.

Were they listening for the changes the boss said he planned to make? Were they distracted by the description of how the boss was dressed? Could they remember how he was dressed or had they tried to put it out of their minds? Did they draw inferences or conclusions concerning the boss's behavior—perhaps about the relationship with his new secretary or his desire to appear more youthful?

Exercise	Message Two: Check Your Listening

Instructions: Read this message aloud to someone one time.

It is the day of a midterm examination in a course called "Listening Effectively." The students have their pens and test booklets ready to write answers for the questions the instructor will ask them. The instructor begins, "Because this is a class in listening, your test will consist of three questions. I will ask them only once. I will not repeat them. After all, this is a course on listening. The first question is: What are the major barriers to listening?"

Just then, there is a commotion in the back of the classroom when a male student pushes another student out of a chair onto the floor and sits in the chair himself. The second student gets up from the floor, yanks the first student's cap from his head, and heads toward the door with the first student in hot pursuit. The instructor shouts at them to stop, but they pay him no heed; in fact, the second student turns and makes an obscene gesture to the instructor and the class. As the other students are trying to grasp what has happened, the teacher continues, "The second question is: What are nine bad habits of listening?"

Finally, the teacher says, "Because listening requires observation, the third question is: Tell in your own words with as much detail as possible what just happened involving the two students who just left the room."

Now have the listener(s) answer these questions:

1. What was the name of the course in which the examination was being given?
2. Were the two students involved in the altercation men or women? (Note: the first was male, but the gender of the other student wasn't mentioned.)
3. What were the three test questions that the instructor asked?
4. What happened as the two students left the room?

Now ask the listener(s) to determine why they could answer some questions better than others.

Were they listening carefully for the questions the instructor asked? Were they distracted by the altercation? Did they ignore the details of the altercation to concentrate on what the instructor was saying? Were they surprised that one of the questions had to do with observing what had happened?

This exercise highlights four characteristics of listening that you should consider.

First, distractions can influence what we hear and how well we listen. In the first message, hearing the reader describe how the boss was dressed may have caused listeners to think about his appearance so much that they did not listen to the boss. In the second message, the altercation may have captured the listeners' attention so much so that they failed to listen for and remember the three test questions the instructor asked.

Second, sometimes we focus our attention and listen so closely for one thing that we fail to attend to another. In the first message, listeners may have been so intent in listening for the three changes the boss planned to make that they failed to grasp the three reasons his employees were having trouble listening to him. With the second message, some listeners may have failed to observe the details of the altercation because they did not want it to distract them. But as the instructor in the story pointed out, observation is an important part of listening effectively.

Third, it is hard to remember all the details of a message when it is stated just once. Repetition aids listening and retention. That's why we are often bombarded with important messages more than once, and they're often delivered in different ways and by different means. For example, when it is time to change to daylight savings time, radio and television stations announce it. Newspapers mention it. And because it happens on a Sunday morning, most church bulletins mention it a week ahead of time.

Fourth, nonverbal cues play an important part in our listening. If you, as listener, could have actually been there when the boss was describing his plans, not only could you have been aided by his nonverbal cues—voice, body language, and so on—you could have seen how he was dressed and how his employees were receiving him. With the second message, you could have listened to the instructor and watched the altercation as well. When the fight broke out in the back of the room, you could have seen what was going on in addition to hearing it. In short, other senses—especially sight—all aid hearing and listening.

Listening with all the senses is important in all situations and contexts. These exercises focused on two of the most critical—the classroom and the job. Surveys show that people who occupy the highest levels in company hierarchies have long recognized the value of listening effectively. CEOs and chief operating officers of companies large and small say poor communication skills are the number-one problem in their organizations. Furthermore, they declare that listening is the communication skill most crucial to success. This is not surprising, for many formal studies have reached the same conclusion: listening is crucial in the workplace.

INSIGHT	*Nobody ever listened himself out of a job.*
	Calvin Coolidge

> *Listening is the single skill that makes the difference between a mediocre and a great company.*
>
> Lee Iacocca

INSIGHT

Listening is also important in other places—in the home, at church, in civic clubs, and at social gatherings. In these and other places, listening to gain information may be less important than listening to improve relationships. Counselors and other experts on interpersonal communication tell us that listening is the skill that can make or break a relationship. To a certain extent, this type of listening is important in the workplace as well; after all, we humans are social creatures, and it is sometimes as important to understand the person as to understand what the person is saying. Even at work, then, there is a lot more to listening than just understanding the meaning of words.

There is no question that listening is both crucial and neglected. The chapters that follow are designed to help you become a better listener in all situations. To do so, you must recognize and eliminate certain false notions and bad habits.

Exercise — Check Yourself: What Kind of Listener Are You?

Do these statements describe you? Check "yes" or "no."

	Yes	No
1. I believe that I am a better listener than most people.	_____	_____
2. I can hear pretty well, so I am probably a good listener.	_____	_____
3. I am a good reader, so it follows that I am a good listener.	_____	_____
4. I am smart, and smart people are generally good listeners.	_____	_____
5. I have become a better listener as I have gotten older.	_____	_____
6. Sometimes I act like I am listening when I am not.	_____	_____
7. If I am not interested in what is being said, I often "tune out."	_____	_____
8. I am easily distracted when trying to listen.	_____	_____
9. If I don't like the speaker or the subject, I find it difficult to listen.	_____	_____
10. I often think about what I plan to say rather than listening to others.	_____	_____

The more "yes" answers you gave, the better the chance that you have some mistaken ideas or bad habits that can be corrected fairly easily. Keep reading to find out how.

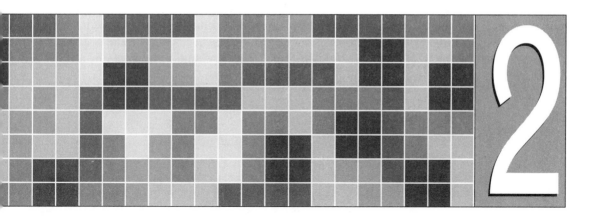

Fallacies About Listening

Objective: Comprehend how fallacies (mistaken ideas) hinder listening.

Tasks: List and explain fallacies about listening.

Give examples showing how each fallacy hinders listening.

Many people have inflated opinions of their own listening performance. Believing that they have no problem with listening, they make no effort to improve. Indeed, why should they? Not knowing that their listening skill is "broke," they see no need to "fix" it. Knowing the following common fallacies about listening will assist you in avoiding them.

FALLACY #1: LISTENING IS NOT MY PROBLEM!

People generally believe they are better listeners than those around them. It is the people they work for or who work with or for them, their own family members, and their friends who have problems listening effectively—not them.

In classes and training seminars, participants are asked to assess themselves as listeners. On a scale of 1 to 10, with 10 being high and 1 being low, they are asked to rate themselves as listeners compared with the other members of the group. The average score through the years has been about 7.5. Some who considered themselves to be really good listeners rated themselves at 9 or 10. Some, of course, rated themselves lower. But the overall spread has not been that great. There is a great tendency for people to rate themselves above average.

Next, they are asked to rate the other group members as listeners. That rating has been 4.1 on average. In other words, they believe that listening is someone else's problem. The people around us believe that we have more of a problem listening effectively than they do. This should tell us something. Listening is not just someone else's problem—it's ours.

You might find it interesting and enlightening to conduct the same activity just described. Use some group you belong to, one where everyone knows each other—a class, a social club, a group of friends, or even a large family. Reproduce the following form and ask them to complete it. Ask participants not to write their names on the forms. Stress that no one will know how anyone else answered. After you have collected all the forms, tabulate the information. You will almost always find that the average of individual rankings will be higher than the average of group rankings. You may wish to share your findings with the group and ask them why they think it turned out that way.

Exercise	How Do You Stack Up?

The ability to listen effectively is one of the things we value most in others and in ourselves. Good listeners are more fun to be around and get along better with others. Think about the other people who are in the group with you. On a scale of 1 to 10, with 1 being lowest and 10 being highest, how would you rate their listening skills? Circle your rating.

1	2	3	4	5	6	7	8	9	10
Lowest				Average listening score for group					Highest

Using the same criteria, rate yourself as a listener.

1	2	3	4	5	6	7	8	9	10
Lowest				Your own listening score					Highest

FALLACY #2: LISTENING AND HEARING ARE THE SAME

Hearing is a prerequisite to listening. If you can't hear, you can't effectively attach meaning to the spoken message. Because the hearing/listening relationship is so important, many textbooks on listening spend a great deal of time discussing the mechanics of hearing—the reception of sound waves, the perception of the sound in the brain, and the auditory association permitting the listener to identify what is being said and what the words mean. Knowing about hearing is worthwhile, but this knowledge will not make you a better listener.

Being blessed with good hearing does not make one a good listener. In fact, many people who have perfectly good hearing are not good listeners, for good listening is not simply hearing the words correctly. You must understand the intended meaning of the words. We communicate effectively with each other insofar as we share meaning. If someone says something to you and you *misunderstand* it, effective communication has not occurred. If someone tells you something and you understand what the person meant, there is effective communication. That is, the symbols have stimulated common meaning and we say that communication is effective. Effective listening implies that the listener understands what the speaker means.

The difference between hearing and listening can be stated this way: *Hearing is the reception of sound; listening is the attachment of meaning to the sound.* Mere hearing is passive; effective listening is active. Understanding the difference between hearing and listening is an important prerequisite for listening effectively.

Read the boxed story on the following page, then ask yourself, "Which kind of job applicant would I have been? Would I have been a listener, or just a hearer?"

Would you have been the person who listened, or would you have been, like most people, a mere hearer? Would you have been the person who got the job? There are always jobs for people who can listen. Employers put a premium on good listening. You won't be listening for the meaning of dots and dashes, but you will be listening for the verbal and nonverbal symbols the speaker uses. You want to listen, not just hear.

FALLACY #3: GOOD READERS ARE GOOD LISTENERS

The statement that good readers are good listeners is often untrue, even though both reading and listening depend on the translation of words into meaning. Because of this shared translation function, listening and reading are obviously related; the problem is that many people mistakenly believe that all good readers are *necessarily* good listeners. And that is simply not so.

Researchers who administer two different standard reading tests to the same individual find a high positive correlation between the two sets of scores. That is, a person who scores well on one reading test generally scores well on another, whereas a person who scores low on one test tends to score low on another. This is also true with standardized listening tests. Those who score high on one listening test tend to score high on the other; if they score low on one test, they generally score low on the other. Interestingly, however, there is often a surprisingly low correlation between an individual's scores on reading tests and that same person's scores on listening tests. A person may score well on a reading test and poorly on a listening test.

Some years ago an experiment was carried out with several classes. Each class was divided into two groups. Students were randomly assigned to each group, and

Listening, or Just Hearing?

Years ago, before the general public had immediate access to the means of instantaneous message transmission that we take for granted today, the telegraph system was a useful and popular way to transmit messages quickly over long distances.

Older individuals remember going into a telegraph office and hearing the distinctive "dot and dash" noise of messages being sent and received. Some of the busiest offices had several machines, and often more than one message was being received at the same time.

An employer is conducting interviews at a large telegraph office to fill a vacancy for an operator. The applicants are all seated in the waiting room where people come to pick up telegrams sent to them. The secretary comes out to tell applicants that the employer is running late, but that the interviews will soon begin. All the while the sound of dots and dashes can be heard over a loudspeaker. All of the applicants hear them, but most pay little attention. They continue talking to one another or just reading.

Suddenly, one of the applicants jumps up and rushes into the manager's office. Soon he returns smiling.

"I got the job!" he exclaims.

"How did you get ahead of us?" the others ask.

"You might have been considered if you hadn't been so busy talking that you didn't hear the manager's coded message," he replies. "It said, 'The person I need must always be on alert. The first one who interprets this message correctly and comes into my office gets the job.'"

then each half of the class was placed in a separate room. Each student in one room was given a short essay and told to read it once and then place it blank side up on the desk. Students in the other room listened as the paper was delivered as a speech. Students in both rooms were then given identical tests on the material covered.

Certain questions were answered correctly more often by those who read the paper, whereas other questions were answered correctly more often by those who heard it delivered as a speech. This result is really not all that surprising. When we read a document, visual cues—margins, illustrations, and punctuation—become factors in our comprehension. When we listen, the speaker's vocal emphasis, reading style, pauses, and gestures influence our understanding. There is, then, a difference between processing information from the written word and processing it from the spoken word. The fact that some people are better at one than the other demonstrates the fallacy of believing that good readers are *necessarily* good listeners.

Two activities follow. Each validates the truth that effective reading and effective listening do not necessarily go hand in hand. In the first activity, one group will read a passage, and the other will listen to the passage being read aloud. The second activity requires only you and one other person. If you are using this book in a class, you may want to pair up with another member.

Exercise   Activity One: Reading vs. Listening

Use any short text—a short story, a newspaper article, or an essay. Write several questions that test the understanding of the message. Read the passage aloud to one group. Hand copies of the passage to individuals in another group to read just once. Use the same questions to test each group's understanding. In most cases you will find that the method of delivery—listening or reading—influences how individuals do on the test.

Exercise   Activity Two: Reading vs. Listening

Using a favorite newspaper, find two articles in different issues, each of the same type and length and by the same writer. For example, you might use two stories from the sports page (from different days), both about the same length, about the same sport, and by the same writer. Satisfy yourself that they are as nearly equivalent as possible. Read one article to another person and ask that person to summarize what you just said. Afterward, let your partner read the other article once and then summarize it.

Ask which task was easier. Decide which one resulted in the most accurate summary. If the other person is a fellow class member, reverse roles. Using different articles—ones that your classmate has selected—you become the listener for one article and the reader for the other. Again decide which task was easiest and for which you were able to give the most accurate summary.

Discuss with each other the differences between reading a message and hearing it read. What can you conclude about your own listening and reading? Attempt to identify techniques to help you be a better listener. Later in this book, I will provide information to help you.

FALLACY #4: SMART PEOPLE ARE BETTER LISTENERS

This fallacy seems to fly in the face of common sense. Smart people obviously have a greater *capacity* to listen, yet, the belief that smarter people are better listeners is often false. In fact, evidence suggests that the reverse is often true.

Some years ago, a listening test and a standardized IQ test were administered to students in several college classes. The results of the two tests were compared for each student. There was little correlation between listening test results and IQ scores—with one surprising exception: there was an inverse relationship between listening scores and IQ scores for those students having the very highest IQ scores. In other words, the smartest students actually scored lower on the listening test than did many students having lower IQ scores. These results suggest that higher intelligence levels do not necessarily result in better listening among college students who possess the *capacity*—if not always the willingness—to listen. Further, higher intelligence may actually interfere with the listening of the smartest students.

Keep in mind that this study was conducted with a specific group—college students. Most were in their late teens and early twenties. Also, the test did not assess all types of listening. It required that students listen to conversations to gain information and to understand the speaker—what we will refer to in Chapter 5 as informative listening and relational listening. It is quite possible that the smartest students were bored with this test, which could explain their lower performance. Whatever the reasons, smart people are not necessarily better listeners. *But they should be*. Intelligence is an asset for several reasons.

INSIGHT   *Intelligence is only an asset if you use it.*

First, intelligent people are generally more educated. They usually have more formal education, but just as important, they tend to read more on their own, are more inquisitive, and have a broader range of interests. In other words, they learn much outside of formal education channels, and they know more about a wider range of subjects than less intelligent people. They are more conversant in the world of ideas and can, therefore, listen and process new information better than less intelligent people.

Second, intelligent people are not as subject to information overload or confusion when there are competing messages. Level of intelligence is related positively to the ability to focus on one message when other messages are present. For example, those with higher intelligence have more success in concentrating on what a speaker is saying even if there is background noise. Furthermore, they are better able to listen and understand two or more messages at the same time than those with lower intelligence, although this phenomenon is not as pronounced for people operating with slightly below average intelligence.

Third, intelligence is positively related to attention span. The length of our attention span plays a role in how well we listen. Obviously, many variables other than intelligence affect attention span. Some very bright people suffer from attention deficit syndrome, and many intelligent people have simply fallen into bad habits, which will be discussed in the next chapter.

> *"That knot between your ears is more than just a place to hang your hat. Think, boy! Use that brain to think."*
>
> The author's grandfather

INSIGHT

FALLACY #5: LISTENING IMPROVES WITH AGE

Certainly, the capacity or ability to listen and attach appropriate meaning to messages improves with age and experience. But although listening *ability* increases, listening *performance* often declines.

Several studies on the relationship of age to listening behavior tell us that young children are better listeners than adolescents, and early adolescents are better listeners than those in their middle teens. Most parents are not surprised by these findings, but most assume that when individuals reach maturity their listening will improve. Unfortunately, that is not so. Adults can understand more difficult and sophisticated material, but when the messages are adjusted to age and grade level, results show a decrease in effective listening. Most people become poorer listeners as they get older.

As people enter the senior years of life, they often worry about Alzheimer's disease. Certainly, this ailment is no laughing matter. Those who have had family members afflicted with this disease know the heartache and stress it causes—not only to the victim, but also to family and friends. Although we don't know if the disease can be prevented, recent studies indicate a relationship between language skills and Alzheimer's. Put simply, those who throughout their lives have demonstrated better communication skills—writing, speaking, reading, and listening—show less incidence of Alzheimer's in later life. This finding presents good reasons for improving our ability to communicate.

Although senior citizens take the threat of Alzheimer's disease seriously, many joke about "senior moments," or "old-timer's disease." This joshing is usually a recognition that they don't listen or remember as well as they once did. (Consider the boxed example on the following page.)

As most people get older, listening becomes more of a problem. So does remembering, which is dependent on listening. (Chapter 4 tells you how to improve and maintain your memory.) Often people protest, "Well, I am just the kind of listener that I am," suggesting that they can really do nothing to improve. Or they may say, "Some people are just born to be better listeners." But the truth is that the decline in listening and in remembering is not so much due to the aging process as it is the result of learned behavior and bad habits. Chapter 3 will focus on some of those bad habits.

"You Forgot My Toast"

A 90-year-old couple are having problems listening to each other and remembering what the other has said. They decide to go to their doctor to make sure nothing is wrong with them. The doctor assures them that they are okay but suggests that perhaps they should start writing things down during conversations.

Later that night while watching TV the old man gets up from his chair and his wife asks, "Where are you going?"

He replies, "To the kitchen."

She asks, "Will you get me a bowl of ice cream?"

He replies, "Sure."

She then asks him, "Don't you think you should write it down?"

He says, "No, I heard what you said, and I can remember that."

She then says, "I also would like some strawberries on top. You had better write that down."

He says, "I heard you. You want a bowl of ice cream with strawberries."

She replies, "Well, I also would like whipped cream on top. I know you will forget that, so you better write it down."

With irritation in his voice, he says, "I don't need to write that down. I heard you and I can remember that." He then heads into the kitchen.

After about 20 minutes he returns from the kitchen and hands her a plate of bacon and eggs. She stares at the plate for a moment and says, "You forgot my toast."

FALLACY #6: LISTENING SKILLS ARE DIFFICULT TO LEARN

Actually, the skills themselves are not all that difficult to learn, and initial progress is rapid. Still, learning to apply the skills consistently takes hard work, and becoming really proficient takes much time and practice—a lifetime, to be exact. However, the effort is definitely worthwhile.

The final chapter presents 18 instructions for listening (see p. 74)—instructions that work. To get their full benefit, however, it is useful to first consider the bad habits of listening, next to understand the process of listening, and finally to know the major types of listening. Before you move on to the next chapter, check yourself with the following questions.

Exercise — Check Yourself: Which Fallacies Are Hindering You?

We have tried to debunk the six fallacies discussed in this chapter, but could it be that you are not entirely convinced? Think honestly about the following six statements and respond as appropriate.

	No	Not Necessarily	Yes
1. Listening is more of a problem for others than for me.	_____	_____	_____
2. Listening and hearing are the same.	_____	_____	_____
3. Good readers are necessarily better listeners.	_____	_____	_____
4. Smart people are better listeners.	_____	_____	_____
5. As people get older they become better listeners.	_____	_____	_____
6. Listening skills are difficult to learn.	_____	_____	_____

How did you do? I hope you answered "no" or "not necessarily" to each question. If you wavered or answered "yes" to any of the questions, make certain that none of the fallacies is keeping you from being the best listener you can be.

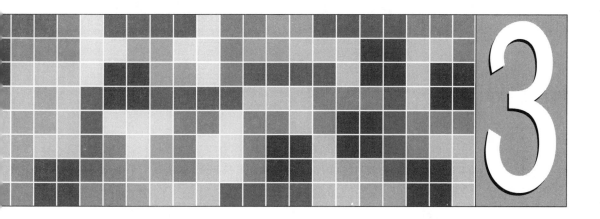

Bad Listening Habits

Objective: Identify bad listening habits that stand in the way of good listening.

Tasks: List and explain bad listening habits.

Give examples of each bad habit.

Explain how each bad habit prevents effective listening.

As you discovered in Chapter 2, bad habits often stand in the way of good listening. In fact, you can make dramatic gains in your listening skills by recognizing and eliminating the bad habits you have. Because habits are learned, they can be changed. That is, they can be "unlearned," and the positive reinforcement for the bad habit can be eliminated.

We learn a lot about not listening while growing up. For example, a parent tells a child, "Don't forget to wear your coat to school!" But the child doesn't want to wear a coat, so the child "learns" to not listen. Later at school, the teacher repeats an assignment several times to make certain that all the students have heard it. The teacher's behavior does not reward the child for listening well the first time, because there will be multiple opportunities to get the message. The repetition in radio and television advertising further conditions us against listening carefully the first time. The bad listening habits we learn as children stay with us into adulthood. Here are nine of the most common bad listening habits.

BAD HABIT #1: THINKING ABOUT WHAT TO SAY RATHER THAN LISTENING TO THE SPEAKER

We are often so interested in planning what we will say that we fail to listen to the person speaking. Then, when we do talk, it sounds as if we weren't listening, which is exactly what has happened.

Duh! Did You Hear What I Just Said?

Professor: "Here is your assignment for next class: I want a three-page paper that expresses your philosophy of leadership. The paper should express your own views and not those of someone else." Just then a student raises his hand and the professor acknowledges him by saying, "Just a minute, Bill. Let me finish giving the assignment; then I will answer your question." The professor continues, "I want you to use the same writing format that you have been using all semester. That is, I want the paper double-spaced, and the typeface should be 12-point Times New Roman. As always, use one-inch margins throughout—at the top and bottom and on the left and right sides. Let me stress again that in this paper you will express your own ideas, not those of anyone else. You will not be citing sources. Now, Bill, what is your question?"

Bill: "Professor, do we use footnotes or endnotes for our sources?"

Bill is not stupid. He did what many people do. He was so focused on what he wanted to say that he failed to listen.

For one day, record examples of individuals who seem to be thinking about what they plan to say rather than listening. Count the number of times this happens to you, either when you are talking or when you should be listening to someone else.

BAD HABIT #2: TALKING WHEN WE SHOULD BE LISTENING

Our entire culture seems to condition us to talk, not to listen. The silent act of listening seems no match for the messages hurled at us almost incessantly. Out-talking others helps us to get our way. Some justify this behavior by saying "the squeaky wheel gets the grease." The truth of the matter is that we miss a lot by talking when we should be listening. And it seems as if some people just can't help themselves.

The Dental Hygienist

Jennifer is a friendly, outgoing person. Everybody likes her. But Jennifer has one very bad habit. She talks too much and has a reputation for dominating every conversation. One day her best friend, Ruiza, takes her aside and says, "Jenn, you know that you are my very best friend, and you probably have more friends than anybody else I know. You are such a giving and caring person, but I need to level with you. Many people get irritated with you because you seem to talk all the time. You don't give others a chance to talk. Why do you do that?"

At first Jennifer is very defensive. Then she says, "Do you know what I think the problem is? As a dental hygienist I have my hands in other people's mouths. They can't talk, so I do. I guess it must just carry over into other areas of my life. Thanks, Ruiza, I will work on keeping quiet so others can talk."

Jennifer had a reason for talking so much. Her practice of talking when her hands were in a patient's mouth had contributed to her habit of talking too much in other situations. In other words, she was *conditioned* to talk too much. A lot of people have this bad habit of talking instead of listening, and they don't have a good reason. The person may have been an only child who received a lot of attention and reinforcement for talking. Or the person may just like to hear the sound of his own voice. Whatever the reasons, talking when we should be listening is a bad habit we need to break. A wise person once observed that because we were created with one mouth and two ears, we should spend twice as much time listening as talking. More of us should heed this advice.

> *The principle of listening is to develop a big ear rather than a big mouth.*   **INSIGHT**
>
> Howard Hendricks

BAD HABIT #3: INTERRUPTING

Interrupting is closely related to talking when we should be listening. It is an extremely irritating habit, and what is so remarkable is that interrupters are often unaware that they are guilty of this bad habit.

People often interrupt because they think that what they have to say is more important than what another person is saying. They may be so focused on their own ideas that they simply tune others out (as in Bad Habit #1). Whatever the reason, interrupters are considered boorish, thoughtless, and lacking in social graces and interpersonal skills.

INSIGHT	*Interrupting others is an annoying and rude habit.*

BAD HABIT #4: LISTENING FOR WHAT WE EXPECT RATHER THAN WHAT IS ACTUALLY SAID

Listening only for what we want to hear becomes a bigger problem as we grow older, and it can create misunderstandings. Whether we are listening to learn, evaluate, discriminate relax, or improve a relationship, it is important to listen to what is actually said.

BAD HABIT #5: PREOCCUPATION WITH OTHER THINGS

Sometimes we don't listen because we are preoccupied. We have so many things to think about—our mind is full of ideas, facts, and worries. In class we find ourselves thinking about everything we have to get done on the weekend or a deadline we have to meet at work. Or our thoughts may be preoccupied with a financial bind we are in or a test we have to take in another course.

On the other hand, our thoughts may be more pleasurable. Perhaps we begin to think about our planned vacation or the date we have next weekend. Sometimes we simply daydream or fantasize, much like James Thurber's character, Walter Mitty. Mitty imagined himself as a hero experiencing great adventures as a surgeon, cowboy, or ship captain—fantasies he would never live out.

Whatever our preoccupations, we must put them aside temporarily if we are to listen effectively. Good listening *demands* that we avoid preoccupation with other things when someone is speaking to us. A characteristic of most CEOs and other successful high-level leaders and managers is that they can focus on the issue at hand. This same quality is found in skilled counselors; they can forget their own concerns to concentrate on the client. Yet, even if you are not a counselor or a manager, the ability to push preoccupation aside is important. Learning requires concentration free from distractions and preoccupation. Learners must listen. Moreover, good relationships require listening that is totally focused on what the other person is saying. If we are preoccupied we cannot listen effectively to friends, family, or coworkers.

BAD HABIT #6: PREJUDICE TOWARD THE SPEAKER OR SUBJECT

Attitudes and feelings not tempered by logic can lead to prejudice. We may not like the speaker. The subject may be one that we know little about and don't care about. We may not like the method of presentation. In any event, we are prejudiced against the presentation—we have prejudged it. Consequently, we

A Confession: I Heard What I Expected to Hear

When my youngest daughter, Missy, was in grade school, she frequently invited girlfriends home with her to eat supper and spend the night. We had four other children in the household at the time, so an extra one or two didn't really bother us. One Saturday, because we were planning to have special guests for the evening meal, I told Missy not to ask anyone home that evening.

"All right," she answered. "May I go to Angie's house this afternoon?"

"I guess so," I said, "if it's all right with Angie's mother. But make certain that you are home by five o'clock."

I didn't think about my conversation with Missy again until about four that afternoon, when the phone rang. I answered it and heard the voice on the other end say, "Hello, Daddy. This is Missy."

I was amused that she called me Daddy and then identified herself, but I decided to play along. "Missy who?" I asked.

"The Missy that lives at your house," she said impatiently. "I'd like to talk to Mama."

"Mama's pretty busy," I informed her. "You'll have to talk to me."

"I'd a whole lot rather talk to Mama," she replied.

With all the parental authority I could muster, I told her, "You will have to talk to me."

There was a slight pause, and then I heard, "Would it be okay for Angie to eat supper and spend the night with us?"

I exploded, "Missy, didn't I tell you that you were not to ask anybody for tonight? I'm coming to get you right now."

"But, Daddy," she pleaded, "it's only four and you said I could stay until five. And besides . . . "

I cut her off, "Besides, nothing. I'm coming now. You be ready!"

I was met at the door by Missy and Angie along with Angie's mother, who said, "John, would it be okay for Missy to eat supper and spend the night with us?"

"Why, that would be nice," I replied.

"But Daddy," Missy piped in, "that's what I just asked you and you told me I couldn't."

"Oh, Missy," I stammered. "I'm sorry. I thought you were asking if Angie could come to our house."

"It's okay," Missy said. "Sometimes you don't listen very well."

As I thought back I knew what had happened. I heard what I expected to hear rather than what Missy actually said.

may mentally argue with the speaker, or we may simply tune out. Prejudicial thinking can divert our attention from what the speaker is saying. And quite often our prejudice is based on inadequate or incorrect information.

What Did You Think of the Speaker?

Tami has purchased tickets for a lecture series on self-improvement and insists that Jimmy go with her to the first lecture. Jimmy does not want to go but agrees to humor Tami. When they get to the lecture hall, Jimmy is so unhappy that he does not even listen to the introduction of the speaker.

When the speaker comes to the lectern, Jimmy leans over to Tami and says, "He looks like that idiot Fred who lives down the street." Tami glares at Jimmy, and he settles back in his seat. As the speaker begins to talk about the importance of physical conditioning, Jimmy thinks to himself, "This guy doesn't look like he is in such hot physical shape. He walks funny; he doesn't have a good presence about him. He even stammers when he talks. Why should I listen to him?" From that point on, Jimmy mentally argues with and discredits everything the speaker says.

On the way home, Tami asks, "What did you think of the speaker?" So Jimmy tells her, belittling and poking fun at the speaker and his message. Tami's response hits Jimmy right between the eyes: "Yes, but he did pretty well for a man who lay in a coma for two months after he lost both legs and his eyesight in combat."

Jimmy's misjudgment of the speaker is a rather extreme example of prejudice, but prejudice is often like this. We make decisions not to listen to a speaker or to discredit the message based on incomplete or incorrect evidence. Jimmy had not listened to the introduction, which explained the speaker's background. Therefore, he judged the speaker unfairly and discredited his message. It's a good policy to suspend judgment about the speaker. Suspend judgment about the speaker, the subject, the treatment of the subject, and anything else that might prejudice your listening.

BAD HABIT #7: TENDENCY TO STEREOTYPE

As thinking and feeling human beings, we hold certain beliefs about a variety of subjects. We have fixed ideas about what is true and correct. If a speaker presents evidence that contradicts our beliefs, we tend to ignore what is being said—either because we find it unbelievable or because we don't want our ideas challenged. Good listeners do not allow themselves to be trapped by their stereotypes.

Both prejudicial listening (Habit #6) and stereotyping can result from listening with a closed mind. A presidential election provides one of the best examples of closed-minded listening. Members of both major parties may listen to the same speeches, but depending on the party affiliation of the candidates and the listeners, the interpretations are often quite different. Our party affiliation influences what we hear. Indeed, research shows that we often do not even bother to listen to the other candidates' messages at all! Likewise, our religious beliefs, cultural heritage, and personal attitudes and values all affect how we listen.

Gender also affects listening. Men and women perceive the world in different ways. Some of these differences are probably due to biological effects, whereas others are due to conditioning. In the United States, boys tend to play games that are more physical, competitive, and results-oriented, perhaps because they are taught to. Girls, on the other hand, tend to play games where winning and losing are less important than the relationships between players.

Listening to men and listening to women are different experiences. Men tend to be more direct in their statements, whereas women use more qualifiers. Consider the difference between "Well, it's about time to think about leaving, isn't it?" and "It's time to leave." The first statement would be made more often by a woman, the second by a man. Women also are more apt to begin a statement with qualifiers such as "I don't know how you feel about this, but . . . " or "I'm not sure everybody agrees with this, but. . . . "

Men and women also listen differently. Women tend to interrupt men less than men interrupt women, and both genders tend to interrupt women more than men. Women seem to focus better on listening, whereas men are more apt to do something else while attempting to listen. Perhaps this is why so many women complain that men just don't listen.

In general, men and women listen differently, and they listen for different things. Now, here is a very important point: *Recognizing the differences can make men and women equivalent listeners*. For example, some would contend that women listen more relationally and men listen more logically. This statement may or may not be true, of course, but the fact remains, if you as a listener take account of your prejudices, stereotypes, strengths, and weaknesses, you can keep these characteristics from limiting your effective listening.

Exercise Determining Possible Prejudices and Stereotypes

Answer each of these questions. If you are reading this book for a class, discuss your answers with four or five other class members. Decide which one of you will share your group's answers with the rest of the class. If you are reading this book on your own, find somebody that you can discuss your answers with.

1. What groups or affiliations have the most impact on how we interpret what we hear? Why?
2. Are these effects positive or negative?
3. Can prejudice ever be good? How about stereotyping?
4. Do you think men and women listen differently? If so, why? If not, why not?

BAD HABIT #8: OUR OWN SELF-CENTEREDNESS

Because we live with ourselves all day every day, most of us spend much more time thinking about ourselves than about others. It is therefore not surprising that self-concern interferes with listening. We must work at transferring our concentration from ourselves to the person doing the talking. The secret of all effective communication, including listening, is to be other-centered.

What? Me? Self-Centered?

I gave a little party
This afternoon at three
'Twas very small
Three guests in all
Just I, myself, and me.
Myself ate up the sandwiches
And drank all the tea
And it was I
Who ate the pie
And passed the cake to me.

BAD HABIT #9: NOT PAYING ATTENTION

This bad habit says it all. In many ways, the other eight bad habits all come down to this. To be a good listener, you have to pay attention.

Do You Have to Pay Attention?

A husband and wife are at a party chatting with some friends about the importance of communication in a marriage.

The husband says, "My wife and I have this communication thing down. She was a communications major in college and I majored in theater arts. She communicates well and I act like I'm listening."

Unfortunately, many people are like the husband in this example. They act like they are paying attention when they are not. Such behavior does not help a relationship, nor does it help the student in the classroom or the worker on the job. Experienced students know the value of paying attention to what the teacher says in class. Usually, what teachers emphasize in class is what they expect students to know for the exam. Spouses know the importance of listening not only to what their partner is saying, but also to what the partner is not saying. Listening up front can prevent serious misunderstandings later. Employees know the value of listening to the boss. Good listening in the office can keep things running smoothly and prevent costly mistakes and misunderstandings. Certainly those in one of the helping professions—such as doctors, nurses, teachers, and counselors—should take special pains to listen. The value of their services depends on listening effectively.

What Did You Say?

A man goes to see a counselor. The counselor asks what he thinks his problem was.

The man tells him, "Nobody pays attention to what I say. My wife doesn't listen, my kids don't listen, nobody at work listens. Nobody listens. What do you think, Doc? What do you think I should do? What do you think, Doc?"

"What did you say?" says the counselor.

If we work to overcome bad habits and are aware of the fallacies about listening, we can make rapid progress in becoming better listeners. But learning to apply the skills consistently does take hard work, and becoming really proficient takes much time and practice—it is a lifetime project. Yet, the effort is definitely worthwhile. Later I will tell you how to become a better listener in any situation. First, however, you need to understand two things: the process of listening and the types of listening. Before we move ahead, take the opportunity to assess your bad habits using the checklist on the following page.

To get the most benefit from the exercise, do the following:

1. Make several copies of the form.

2. Ask someone who knows you well to rate you using the form. You might choose to have several others rate you. Compare your own ratings with theirs. Are there differences? Determine why they rated you differently than you rated yourself.

3. If you are in a class, compare your assessment of yourself with other students' assessment of themselves. (If you are not in a class, ask several friends to rate themselves.) Are some habits more prevalent than others? Discuss how you will approach your bad habits. What steps will you personally take to get rid of these habits? For example, if interrupting is a problem, you may (a) ask your close friends to tell you when they catch you interrupting others, (b) pinch yourself every time you catch yourself interrupting, or (c) record conversations (with the approval of the others involved, of course) so that you can go back and listen to your own interrupting behavior. The point is that if you decide what steps to take

Exercise — What Bad Habits Do You Have?

Rate yourself using the following key:

Usually = 5

Often = 4

Sometimes = 3

Seldom = 2

Never = 1

1. You think about what you want to say rather than listening to what is being said. _____

2. You talk when you should listen. _____

3. You interrupt others when they are talking. _____

4. You hear what you expect to hear rather than what is actually said. _____

5. Your preoccupation with other things hinders listening. _____

6. Your prejudice against the speaker or subject hinders your listening. _____

7. Your tendency to stereotype keeps you from maintaining an open mind. _____

8. Your self-centeredness keeps you from focusing on what others are saying. _____

9. For whatever reason, you don't pay attention to what others are saying. _____

Total score _____

How did you do?

9–14 Wow! That's impressive. Are you sure you aren't kidding yourself?

15–22 Not too bad, but you can improve.

23–30 You've got some work to do. Do it, and you will make great improvement.

31–45 There is no way but up. Cheer up! We all have to start somewhere.

to overcome a bad habit, you will be more successful than if someone else tries to solve the problem for you. Taking ownership of the problem and committing yourself to work on it will help you overcome or reduce the bad habit. Attack each bad habit you have, and you will be on your way to becoming a better listener.

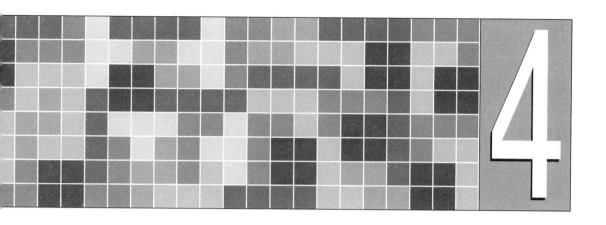

The Listening Process

Objective: Analyze the listening process so that you will be a more effective listener.

Tasks: Discuss the parts of the listening process.

Explain how selectivity, strength, and sustainability of attention influence listening.

Explain how verbal and nonverbal barriers hinder effective listening.

Listening is an important but often ignored part of the communication process. This neglect results largely from two factors. First, speaking and writing (the sending parts of the communication process) are highly visible and are more easily assessed and tested than listening and reading (the receiving parts). Second, many of us seem unwilling to improve our listening skills, perhaps because we don't understand the process. Understanding the process will help us know how to improve.

To understand the listening process, we must first define it: Listening is the process of receiving, attending to, and understanding what people are saying. We should also consider two additional steps that are often present in the process: responding and remembering. The process moves through the key steps—receiving, attending, and understanding—in sequence. Responding and/or remembering may or may not follow. For example, it may be desirable for the listener to respond immediately or to remember the message and respond at a later time. On the other hand, it is possible that neither responding nor remembering will occur. At times, no response (at least no overt response) is required, and the act of remembering may or may not be necessary. For example, if someone tells you to watch your step, you have no need to remember the message after you have acted upon it.

The best way to understand the process is to look at the five parts of the process one at a time. The following sections will draw an analogy between the listening process and the electronic mail (e-mail) system. Suppose that you are the sender of a message and I am the intended recipient.

RECEIVING

This step, receiving, is easily understood. You send an e-mail message to me. It may be well composed and clear. You may have used effective techniques to organize and support your message. The subject may be one of great interest to me. Moreover, I like to receive e-mail from you. In short, you have done a good job and I want to receive the message. But if I don't turn on my computer, I won't receive it. The message remains somewhere between your computer and mine, between sender and receiver.

Much human listening fails for the same reason. Receivers simply are not connected or tuned in to the senders. Sometimes, the problem is a physiological one; for example, the receiver has a hearing deficiency due to a congenital or inherited weakness. Or the deficiency may be the result of an accident, a disease, or prolonged exposure to loud noises. Sometimes the problem can be corrected through medical or surgical intervention or through hearing aids. Scientists and engineers are constantly developing new products designed to correct and help specific types of hearing loss.

Remember that hearing and listening are not the same. Hearing is the reception of sound; listening is the attempt to attach meaning to the sound. Hearing or reception is, however, a necessary prerequisite for listening and an important component of the listening process.

ATTENDING

Let's continue with the e-mail analogy as we look at the second part of the listening process. When I turn my computer on, it will receive the message that you sent. But I must do more. I must pay attention to the message if the process is to continue. If I leave my desk to take a phone call just after I turn on my computer, I will not know that you have sent a message. Or I may not have an opportunity to read my e-mail that day. Suppose I am working on something else when the message arrives. My computer signals that I have mail from you. I want to read it, but I decide that I will do it later. I continue to stay busy on another task and forget to read the message. Later, I may mistakenly delete it without ever reading it. Whatever the case, I don't attend to the message. Human listening is often ineffective—or does not occur—for similar reasons. Receiving occurs, but attending does not.

At any given time, numerous messages compete for our attention. The stimuli may be external, such as words spoken by a lecturer or printed on paper. Or the stimuli may be internal, such as a deadline we must meet tomorrow, a backache we developed from sitting too long at the computer, or the hunger pangs we experience because we didn't take time to eat lunch. Whatever the source of the stimuli, we simply can't focus on all of them at the same time. We choose, whether consciously or unconsciously, to attend to some stimuli and reject others. Three factors determine how these choices are made: selectivity of attention, strength of attention, and sustainability of attention.

Selectivity of Attention

We focus our attention to make sense of an information overload. For example, suppose you are attempting to read a book and watch TV at the same time. Although some people claim they can do this, actually both activities suffer— and usually one more than the other. The material that is most engaging or interesting will dominate your attention. Selectivity of attention explains why you perk up when something familiar to you, such as your hometown or your favorite hobby, is mentioned. You may be listening intently to one conversation when someone in a different conversation mentions your name. Immediately, the focus of your attention shifts to the conversation in which your name was mentioned.

That's More Interesting Than What I Was Saying?

One day in 1973 I was lecturing to a thousand college students enrolled in the basic communication course. At this time, the fad of streaking—in which a stark-naked (or nearly naked) student unexpectedly dashes through a gathering of people—had hit the campus. On that particular day, near the end of the lecture a streaker dressed only in combat boots and a football helmet ran across the stage. Needless to say, I lost the attention of the audience. I tried for several minutes to regain their attention, and then finally decided to dismiss the class early. I had always believed that I was a good lecturer and could hold the audience's attention, no matter what. I was wrong!

Strength of Attention

Attention is not only selective; it possesses energy and strength. People who try to read a book and watch TV at the same time find that sooner or later they are directing stronger attention toward either the book or the TV. Strong attention can generally be given to only one stimulus at a time. Even if someone is able to both read and watch TV at the same time, there is a limit to how many things a person can do at once. If we spend too much energy on too many stimuli, the strength of attention toward each one of them will suffer and we will not be paying much attention to any of them. We have all been in situations where too much was happening for us to comprehend it all. We usually focus the strength of our attention on one thing.

Consider how we can be so attentive to a newspaper, a TV program, a personal computer, a sports event, or another individual that we are oblivious to our surroundings. Watch a young couple in love, and you'll see a good example of intensity, or strength of attention.

Another measure of attention strength is the length of time that the memory of an event or person continues to influence us. I still remember vividly the sermon preached at my grandfather's funeral—a rendering of Martin Luther King, Jr.'s "I Have a Dream" speech—and the one and only time I heard President Ronald Reagan speak in person. I remember them because they had my full attention.

Sustainability of Attention

Attention cannot be sustained indefinitely. Our attention wanes, and this fact is important to an understanding of listening. For example, we can listen to some public speakers far longer than we can listen to others. Duration of attention may depend on the subject, the setting, the way the speech is packaged, and the speaker's delivery. Even if the speaker is articulate and skilled and the content is interesting, our attention finally ends. If for no other reason, the human body has physical needs, such as sleep, that must be met. The mind can only pay attention for as long as the body can sit still.

INSIGHT   *The mind can only attend to what the body can endure.*

UNDERSTANDING

Someone once said, "Successful communication begins with understanding." How true! A message may have been sent and received, and the receiver may have attended to the message—yet, there may not have been effective communication. Effective communication does not take place until the receiver *understands* the message.

> *Man's inability to communicate is a result of his failure to listen effectively, skillfully, and with understanding to another person.*
>
> Carl Rogers

INSIGHT

Let's return to the e-mail analogy. Suppose I receive the e-mail message, open it, and read it. Has effective communication occurred? Not necessarily. Even though I read every word of your message, I might not understand what you meant.

There are several possible reasons for the misunderstanding. I may have expected the message to say something that it didn't say, so my understanding is more in line with my expectations than what it actually said. We often hear or read what we expect rather than what was actually said or written (as was illustrated earlier in the story about Missy). Perhaps the real point of the message was obscured by other information and I missed the point. In listening, the key point is sometimes missed. A worker tells a supervisor what happened while the supervisor was out of the office. While relating all the events, the worker mentions that the supervisor's boss asked that the supervisor call upon her return. The supervisor misses this important piece of information because her attention is focused on other parts of the message. Later, the supervisor asks the worker why he failed to tell her that her boss wanted to see her. But the worker *had* told her; the supervisor just hadn't understood.

Our expectations and/or our failure to get the point often lead to misunderstanding, but the major reason I don't understand the e-mail is probably something else—the words you used and the manner in which you arranged them. Neither of us was necessarily at fault; we simply attached different meanings to the words. We communicate effectively with each other only insofar as we share similar meanings for the same verbal or nonverbal symbols that we are using. With e-mail, the message is limited to words or other visual symbols that represent words. In listening, both verbal and nonverbal symbols are crucial to understanding. In the following sections, we will consider the roles verbal and nonverbal symbols play.

Verbal Symbols

Verbal communication means communicating through the use of words, whether spoken or written. Two barriers obstruct our understanding of verbal communication.

Barrier #1: The same words can mean different things to different people. This barrier, a common one, may be experienced whenever two people attempt to communicate. I may tell my colleague that the temperature in the office is quite comfortable. My "quite comfortable," however, is her "uncomfortable." For me, 78 degrees is comfortable; for her, 65 degrees is comfortable. The same word can mean different things to different people. A friend tells me he will be over in five minutes. To him, five minutes means "soon"—perhaps any time in the next half hour. I, on the other hand, attach a literal meaning: five minutes means five minutes.

Which Circle Drive Are You Talking About?

Some years ago when I was a professor of speech communication at the University of Missouri in Columbia, I called my wife and asked her to pick me up at the circle drive near Switzler Hall, where my office was located. I wasn't thinking very clearly, for there were two circle drives. One was a handy little circle that came right up to the back door. The other was a larger, more impressive drive that came within 50 yards of the front door. People often drove up the front drive to get a scenic view of the old red-brick campus.

Well, you guessed it. I went to the smaller, less impressive drive. My wife went to the larger one. At about the same time we both figured out what happened. I came around to the front of the building just in time to see her pull away. Even then I didn't guess where she was headed. After a few trips back and forth, we finally got together. Since then, one of us asks, "Just which circle drive are you talking about?"

Having a Ph.D. in communication does not mean that I always communicate effectively. Here is what I learned that day at the university: to consider what the words mean to the other person, not only what they mean to me.

Usually, only minor irritation results from such differences, but sometimes the consequences can be more severe. Consider the following information given me by a fire inspector. The fire inspector said that workers exhibit great caution when they are working around gasoline drums. They take great care not to smoke or ignite matches nearby. But when the drums are emptied and labeled "empty gasoline drums," caution is thrown to the wind. Workers feel comfortable striking matches and smoking cigarettes in the area. Ironically, vapors that emanate from "empty" drums are much more volatile than liquid gasoline. The word *empty* has a different meaning for the workers than for the experienced fire inspector, who knows the potential for disaster is present. Sometimes the misunderstanding of one word's meaning can lead to tragic consequences as the box on the following page indicates. Whether the possible consequences are disastrous or not, it is important to listen carefully and to listen as much as possible from the speaker's perspective.

Barrier #2: Different words can mean the same thing. Many things are called by more than one name. Two men who are working in Boston go to a

A Traveler's Tragic End

A traveler stops at a convenience store to ask directions. The man behind the counter points to a traffic signal a block away and says, "Go to that intersection, take an immediate left, and go about a mile. It will be the big red building on your right."

The traveler repeats, "Go to the traffic light, take an immediate left, and go a mile to the red building on my right. Is that it?"

"That's right," says the clerk.

Unfortunately, the traffic light is on the corner heading into the intersection, and the man in the store had neglected to mention the grassy median that separates northbound and southbound lanes. The traveler takes an "immediate left" and heads south in the northbound lane. Less than one block later he slams headfirst into an 18-wheeler and is killed.

restaurant. One of the men is a native Bostonian; the other has recently transferred there from the Midwest. The Midwesterner tells the waiter that he would like some pop to drink. The waiter doesn't understand until the Midwesterner says, "You know, pop. It comes in a bottle or a can; you shake it and it fizzes." The waiter says, "Oh! You mean a soda." But *soda* means something else to the Midwesterner. He thinks of an ice cream soda from a soda fountain. There are a few more moments of confusion until the waiter and the Midwesterner understand one another. *Soft drink*, *soda*, and *pop* all mean the same thing when used in the same context. The name used depends on who is doing the talking.

Did you ever wonder just how many words in the English language have more than one meaning? For a starter, consider that the 500 most commonly used words in our language have a total of about 15,000 definitions—an average of 30 per word. The following sentence serves as an illustration:

Fred has been crestfallen since he fell out of favor with the Fall Festival Committee last fall, after he had a falling out with Frank because Frank had fallen in with a new crowd of people rather than falling in love with Fred's sister, Fallina.

Not a great sentence, but it illustrates a few of the more than 50 meanings of *fall*. Our language is marked by its multiusage. If you doubt it, describe some object or animal in detail to several talented artists and ask them to draw what you describe. Chances are that each one will draw a distinctively different picture. Try it for yourself. Draw several geometrical figures on a page—perhaps a circle, a rectangle, and a couple of triangles. Then, without showing them the picture you have drawn, instruct the rest of the class (or any group of people) on how to draw a picture identical to yours, down to the placement of the figures on the page. Their listening and understanding will be challenged, and your frustration level will rise. Try it; you'll see.

These two barriers—one word having several meanings and different words having the same meaning—can be overcome if you realize the following: meanings are not in words; meanings are in people. We listen more effectively when we consider the message in relation to its source. Good listeners always consider who the sender of the message is. Knowing something about the sender pays big dividends when it comes to listening and understanding verbal messages.

Nonverbal Symbols

In oral communication, nonverbal symbols often transmit even more information than verbal symbols. We communicate nonverbally in three ways—through action factors, nonaction factors, and vocal factors. Each factor is associated with a barrier to listening.

Barrier #1: Misinterpretation of the action. Body language, eye contact, gestures, and facial expression are action factors that affect the meaning we attach to an oral message. For that matter, any movement or action carries meaning. Studies show that we listen better to speakers who use effective eye contact. There are at least two reasons. First, these speakers seem to be interested in us, and we listen better to people we think are interested in us. Second, they appear more credible to us. The more effectively speakers use eye contact with their audiences, the more credible audiences think they are and the better audiences listen. But the danger of misinterpretation of nonverbal symbols always exists. For example, speakers may look away and we wrongly conclude they are not interested in us. Or they may move toward us in an attempt to build rapport and we consider the movement threatening.

In everyday situations at school, on the job, and with friends or family, when someone walks quickly away from a conversation or taps a pencil on the desk during a conversation, we may conclude that the person is in a hurry or is bored. Our conclusions may or may not be correct. We may conclude that speakers who twitch or otherwise seem unsure are nervous when, in fact, they may not be. Beware of misinterpreting the actions of others. Also, beware of letting poor delivery skills influence your judgment of the speaker's message. Some speakers may not use effective eye contact, gestures, or facial expressions, but may still have much worthwhile information to share. Other speakers have good delivery skills but don't have much worthwhile to say.

Barrier #2: Misinterpretation of nonaction symbols. The clothes I wear, the automobile I drive, and the objects in my office communicate information about me. In addition, whether or not I respect your time and personal space affects how you interpret my messages. For example, if I have an appointment to see you at noon but arrive 15 minutes late, my tardiness may adversely affect how you interpret what I say to you. If I crowd you—get too close to you physically or emotionally—you may tune me out. However, although my possessions and other nonverbal cues may communicate certain information to you, your interpretation may not be correct. Effective listeners take pains to not misinterpret nonaction symbols.

Barrier #3: Misinterpretation of the voice. The quality, intelligibility, and variety of the speaker's voice affect the listener's understanding. Quality refers to the overall impression the voice makes on others. Listeners often infer from the voice whether the speaker is happy or sad, fearful or confident, excited or bored. Intelligibility depends on such things as articulation, pronunciation, and grammatical correctness. Variety is the spice of speaking. Variation in rate, volume, force, pitch, and emphasis influences understanding of the speaker's message. Vocal delivery and, especially, variations in the voice are important because they can help us determine meaning. But misinterpreting vocal cues is always a possibility, which is why effective listeners assess all cues, both verbal and nonverbal.

RESPONDING

Technically, the listening process could end with understanding, for effective listening may be defined as the understanding of meaning. But a response may be needed—or at least be helpful. There are several types of responses.

Responses that comply. These responses may be spoken or written. Let's continue with the e-mail analogy. After I have received, attended to, and understood the message you sent, I may respond, particularly if you asked a question. Perhaps you requested that I call or visit you, in which case I would do so. Or you might have asked me to think about an issue and give you some advice, in which case I could send a quick e-mail indicating that I will get back to you later. So it is in listening. Often a direct verbal response is required, or at least desired. Such a response indicates compliance with the other's wishes.

Responses that seek clarification. I may use e-mail to ask for additional information, or I may talk to you on the telephone or face-to-face. I may be very direct in my request, or I may just say, "Tell me more about it." Often when we are speaking, people ask for clarification or their nonverbal reaction shows that clarification is needed.

Responses that paraphrase. I may say something like, "In other words, what you are saying is. . . ." A paraphrase gives the sender a chance to agree or to clarify.

Nonverbal responses. Many times a nonverbal response is all that is needed; indeed, it may even be the preferred type of response. The knowing nod of the head, an understanding smile, or a "thumbs up" may communicate that the message is understood.

Responding, then, is a form of feedback that completes the communication transaction. It lets the sender know that the message was received, attended to, and understood.

REMEMBERING

Memorization of facts is not the key to good listening, yet a good memory is often an asset in the listening process. Some would go so far as to say, "If you can't remember it, you weren't listening." Of course, this statement is often untrue. Think, for example, of the times you hear a good joke but can't remember it long enough to get home and tell it, or the number of times you go to the grocery store and can't remember what you were asked to buy, and the most frustrating situation of all—you are introduced to someone and can't recall the name five minutes later. We often say, "I can remember faces, but I can't remember names." At times, something will jog our memory, such as hearing another joke, seeing a similar product on the grocery store shelf, or meeting someone else with the same first name.

What is the relationship between memory and listening? Understanding the differences between short-term memory and long-term memory will help explain the connection. With short-term memory, information is used immediately—within a few seconds, for example, as with a phone number that we look up. Often we only have to remember the information for a few seconds or minutes—perhaps just long enough to follow some instructions. Or we may remember material only long enough to be tested over it. In such cases, a good short-term memory can serve us well.

Long-term memory, on the other hand, allows us to recall information and events hours, days, weeks—even years—later. You remember, for example, what happened to you when you were growing up, songs you learned, people you knew. You may have been unaware of those memories for long periods of time, and then the right stimulus caused you to recall them. Perhaps the aroma of a freshly baked pie called to mind your grandmother, who used to make great apple pies years ago. It's funny how things like that will come back to you.

Remembering becomes a very important component of the listening process if you will need the information later. Listening and remembering skills go hand in hand. Think back to the story in Chapter 2 about the elderly man bringing back the wrong thing to his wife from the kitchen. I emphasized that often memory loss is blamed when actually poor listening is the culprit.

Memory is like a muscle. The more it is used, the better it gets. The more it is neglected, the worse it gets. While we are in school or engaged in a job that requires us to use our memories intensively to remember facts, pass exams, or apply what we have learned, our mind and our memory are challenged. When

"It'll All Come Back To Ya"

A minister retires and moves to the country to enjoy life and practice his hobby of yard work. Needing a lawn mower, he heads into town to buy one. On the way he sees a sign advertising a lawn mower for sale. He stops at the house and a young lad comes out to greet him. The minister asks about the lawn mower and the kid says it is behind the house. The two go to look at the lawn mower. The engine is sputtering along at idle speed. The preacher increases the speed of the engine and mows a few strips. Satisfied that the mower will do the job, he agrees to a price of $25.

Later in the day, the young lad is riding his bicycle when he spies the minister pulling on the engine starter rope. The kid stops and watches for a couple of minutes. He asks, "What's wrong?"

The minister replies, "I can't get this mower started. Do you know how?"

The kid says, "Yep."

"Well, how do you do it? Tell me!" the minister yells.

The kid replies, "You have to cuss it."

The minister rises up indignantly. "Now you listen here. I am a minister and if I ever did cuss, not saying I have, I've forgotten how to do it after all these years."

With a wise look on his face well beyond his years, the kid says, "Preacher, you keep on pulling that rope and it'll all come back to ya."

we leave school for a job that no longer challenges us or retire from a mentally demanding job, memory will decline dramatically if it is not stimulated in some way. Memory works by linking information and fitting facts and information into mental frameworks. The more you are engaged in actively remembering, the more information and frameworks you have, and additional ideas and facts will fit into those frameworks.

A related reason that memory declines outside of academia or jobs is that information is no longer received in such a structured manner. Clear presentation of information in a classroom or training course and predictable routines on the job provide structures that aid memory. In other words, the framework of school or a job makes it easier to link information.

Memory in most people gets worse with age because it is allowed to. Continue your education throughout life. Cultivate your mind. Keep it open to new experiences. Adjust to change. Fit new facts and information you learn into clear frameworks. Keep learning and keep challenging your memory and, barring medical problems, it won't fail you. Neglect your memory and it will begin to leave you. The following sections present five techniques you can use to improve memory.

Repetition

This method is the most basic way to remember a list of items. Simply recite the list over and over. For example, you are going to the grocery store to buy soap, cereal, bleach, soup, bread, salsa, a mop, paper towels, jelly, orange juice, beets, and milk. You don't have a pen and paper to write it down. By reciting the list over and over, you hope to remember it until you get to the store and purchase the items. Although repetition is often useful for short-term retention, it is also an important explanation for long-term retention. When we remember events that happened to us years ago, the thought seldom comes to us after having lain dormant in our minds for a long period of time, although such things do happen. Something can trigger a memory of things long past, but most often we remember events from years ago because we have thought about them many times since they happened. Remembering keeps the memory alive.

Chunking

Most people can repeat and remember three to five pieces of information. Experienced public speakers who know this fact will seldom have over three or four main points to their speech so that the audience can remember all of them. Chunking takes advantage of this fact by grouping items into inclusive chunks or categories. For example, the grocery list given above might be grouped as follows: breakfast items—cereal, milk, orange juice, bread (for toast), and jelly; canned goods—beets, soup, and salsa; and cleaning items—paper towels, soap, bleach, and mop. Now there are three lists to remember, each with five or fewer items. With chunking, your chance of remembering all the items that you want from the store will be much better.

Patterning

Identifying logical patterns can aid memory. Sometimes things that begin with the same letter or sound can be grouped together. This tactic can aid remembering. I wanted to stress the importance of selectivity of attention, intensity of attention, and duration of attention. Knowing that the terms *selectivity*, *intensity*, and *duration* might be difficult to remember, I renamed two of these categories. *Intensity* became *strength*. *Duration* became *sustainability*. Now the three points all start with the same letter and have parallel structure—selectivity of attention, strength of attention, and sustainability of attention. Identifiable patterns aid memory.

Association

Various methods of association can help us link what we want to remember with what we already know. Sometimes these associations are very simple. I have a combination lock with the numbers 16, 42, and 5. Here is how I remember it. I got my driver's license at age 16, I ran my fastest 10K race at age 42, and I have 5 children. It works for me.

Names present a special challenge for most people. Suppose you meet a person named Adam Johnson. You remember that the second president of the United States was named John Adams. You might even say to Adam Johnson, "Your name should be easy to remember; I will just associate your name with that of the second president, John Adams." A man named Bill Wojchiechowski knows that people have trouble pronouncing and remembering his name. He makes it easy. He tells people, "Just say 'watch ya house key.'" People remember Bill Wojchiechowski's last name easier than his first. That's okay. When they meet him they can say, "Hello, Mr. watch ya house key." He can say, "Just call me Bill."

Another method of association is to think of a linking word. For instance, the word *patriotism* links the Pledge of Allegiance, the National Anthem, the Fourth of July, and Veterans Day. You can create your own word links that will be meaningful to you. If you need to remember a picture frame, a baseball bat, a chair, and toothpicks, you might think of the word *wood*. If you are an abstract thinker, the word *spring* might provide the connection to remember a bed (it has springs), a watch (they all used to have springs), and a reference book (wellspring of information). The point is to create a link that helps you remember.

Visualization

Most information is processed through either auditory or visual channels. Many speakers use graphics and PowerPoint slides to visually aid in their presentation of materials. Listeners also have the ability to create their own visual aids in their minds. When someone describes a red convertible with a young man and woman speeding down the interstate, the listener may construct a mental picture. Visualization helps the listener remember information. The more detailed and specific the visualization, the better it is as a memory aid.

Listeners need to do everything possible to improve their ability to remember, for remembering is a very important part of the listening process. Before moving on to types of listening, see how you answer a few questions about the listening process (see the box on the following page).

Figure 4.1 on the following page summarizes the listening process.

Discuss these questions in class. If you are reading this book on your own, share what you have learned in this chapter with some friends and discuss these questions with them. Hearing their feedback may help you commit to becoming a better listener.

1. What techniques do speakers use that hold your attention?
2. In a conversation, what helps you keep your attention focused?
3. Think of a speech, lecture, or program you have recently listened to. How did selectivity, strength, and sustainability played a part in your attention and how you listened?
4. This chapter discussed two verbal barriers and three nonverbal barriers to listening. What are some examples of each of these from your own experience?
5. What determines whether or not responding is necessary or desired?
6. What steps will you take to ensure that your memory does not deteriorate?
7. What techniques do you use to remember? What new ones have you learned?

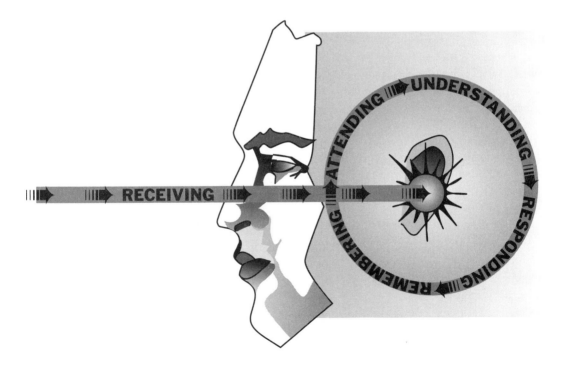

Figure 4.1   The listening process.

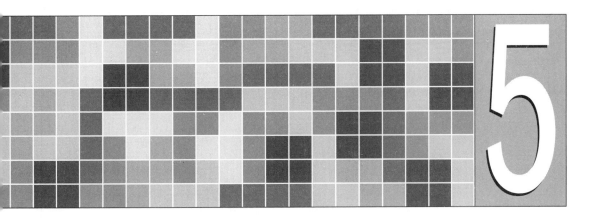

Types of Listening

Objective: Analyze the five types of listening and learn skills appropriate to each type.

Tasks: Describe the five types of listening.

Discuss the influence of vocabulary, concentration, and memory on informative listening.

Discuss the role of attending, supporting, and empathizing in relational listening.

Discuss the effects of presentation, perception, and previous experience on appreciative listening.

Discuss the importance of ethos, logos, and pathos to critical listening.

Discuss the importance of hearing ability, sound structure, and nonverbal cues to discriminative listening.

Different situations require different types of listening. We may listen for pleasure, to get information, to improve a relationship, to make a critical judgment, or to discriminate among verbal or nonverbal symbols. Understanding the five basic types of listening will help us apply the instructions for listening given in Chapter 6.

INFORMATIVE LISTENING

Informative listening is listening in which the listener's primary concern is simply to understand what the other person is saying. Listeners are successful insofar as the meaning they assign to messages is as close as possible to that which the sender intended.

Informative listening is found in all areas of our lives. Much of our learning involves informative listening to lectures. In the workplace, we listen to understand new procedures, and how well we perform depends on how well we listen. We listen to instructions, briefings, reports, and speeches; if we listen poorly, we aren't equipped with information we may need.

At times, careful informative listening is absolutely crucial, as you learned in the Chapter 1 anecdote about the aircraft landing. At other times, careless listening results in only aggravation or misunderstanding, as in my conversation with Missy described in Chapter 3. Whatever the situation, effective informative listening demands that you concentrate squarely on the message, including its source.

Experienced students know that good listening saves time. They have learned that few things not covered in class will be on tests. For this reason alone it is difficult to understand why some students do not think attendance is important. At no time was this message brought home more clearly than when I was an undergraduate.

I was taking a course required for students in many disciplines. In this course, the entire grade rested on the midterm and final examinations. For many years the professor had used the same text, and he had the reputation of always testing from what was in the book rather than what was in the lecture. He even stated that his lectures were only for the students' "enrichment." This statement had come to mean that information in lectures was not testable. Because attendance was never taken in the course, usually only about a fourth of the students would regularly attend lectures—those who wanted the "enrichment."

During the last week of the course the professor became ill. His graduate teaching assistant (GTA) gave the final lecture and announced that he would also be giving the final examination. We all assumed that the professor had already prepared the examination and that the GTA would merely be proctoring the exam. I studied what I had underlined from the textbook, and then more for amusement than anything else, I quickly looked back over my lecture notes—the ones that were for my "enrichment."

At the final exam I saw students whom I had seen in the course only twice before—on the first day of class and at the midterm examination. Imagine my surprise—and theirs—when they began the test. Four of the five questions required knowledge of information that came only from the lecture. The GTA had asked and received permission from the professor to prepare and grade the test. I was lucky that day. I might have been one of those students who had skipped lectures. I was fortunate to have listened in class, taken notes, and reviewed them the night before the exam. Since then, I have always tried to listen. You never know when that information may be on a test.

Living life is a lot like going to school. Listen carefully, because it may be on a test. **INSIGHT**

Effective informative listening relies on vocabulary, concentration, and memory. Work on these and you will improve your informative listening skills.

Vocabulary

The precise relationship between vocabulary and listening has never been determined, but it is clear that increasing your vocabulary will increase your understanding. It's never too late to improve your vocabulary. Cultivating a genuine interest in words and language, making a conscious effort to learn new words, and breaking down unfamiliar words into their components will help you improve your vocabulary.

A good way to improve your vocabulary is to be sensitive to the context in which words are used. Sometimes, unfamiliar words appear with synonyms: Her attractive, *winsome* personality won us over. At other times, a contrast is drawn: He is usually quite energetic, but today he seemed *lethargic*. Occasionally, an unfamiliar word is used to summarize a situation or quality. Consider this assessment of a quarterback's performance in a football game: He passed for over 200 yards, ran for 50 more, and his three punts averaged over 45 yards; he turned in a *stellar* performance. Look for contextual clues to help you learn new words and improve your vocabulary.

Perhaps the best way to improve your vocabulary is to learn one new word each day. That's 365 words each year. In three years you will have learned over a thousand new words, more new words than many people have in their entire vocabularies.

Concentration

Concentration is difficult. We are all guilty of poor concentration at some time. Sometimes listeners try to divide their attention between two competing stimuli. At other times, listeners are preoccupied with something other than the speaker. Sometimes listeners are too concerned with their own needs to concentrate on the message being delivered. They may lack curiosity, energy, or interest. Many people simply have not learned to concentrate while listening. Others refuse to discipline themselves, lacking the motivation to accept responsibility for good listening. Concentration requires discipline, motivation, and acceptance of responsibility.

Whoops! I Don't Think I Heard What You Said

Teri interrupts her father's reading of the newspaper to ask, "Is it okay if I take your car over to a friend's house to spend the night? I'll be home before you go to work in the morning." Without concentrating on what she is asking, her father says, "Sure, go ahead." Several minutes later, he realizes what Teri said. She is not coming home that night, and he has to leave the house earlier than usual the next morning for a breakfast meeting where he is briefing some clients. All of his notes, his computer, his projector, and his PowerPoint slides are in the automobile. Fortunately, he is able to track down his daughter and retrieve his automobile and its contents.

Memory

Memory was discussed in detail in Chapter 4, but it deserves mention again here. Memory is especially crucial in informative listening; you cannot process information without bringing memory into play. Memory helps your informative listening in three ways. First, it allows you to recall experiences and information necessary to function in the world around you. Without memory you would have no knowledge bank. Second, it establishes expectations about what you will encounter. You would be unable to drive in heavy traffic, react to new situations, or make common decisions in life without memory. Third, it allows you to understand what others say. Without simple memory of the meaning of words, you could not communicate with anyone else. Without memory of concepts and ideas, you could not understand the meaning of messages.

RELATIONAL LISTENING

The purpose of relational listening is either to help an individual or to improve a relationship. Therapeutic listening is a special type of relational listening. Therapeutic listening is used in situations where counselors, medical personnel, or other professionals allow a troubled person to talk through a problem. But it can also be used when you listen to friends or acquaintances "get things off their chests." Although relational listening requires you to listen for information, the emphasis is on understanding the other person. Three behaviors are key to effective relational listening: attending, supporting, and empathizing.

Attending

Chapter 4 addressed the importance of paying attention, or *attending*. In relational listening, attending behaviors indicate that the listener is focusing on the speaker. Nonverbal cues are crucial in relational listening; they indicate that you are attending to the speaker—or that you are not!

> **INSIGHT**
>
> *She was the kind of listener that storytellers love. She nodded her head in all the right places.*
>
> Margaret Drake

Eye contact is one of the most important attending behaviors. Looking appropriately and comfortably at the speaker sends a message that is vastly different from that sent by a frequent shifting of gaze, staring, or looking around the room. Body positioning communicates acceptance or lack of it. Leaning forward, toward the speaker, demonstrates interest; leaning away communicates lack of interest. Head nods, smiles, frowns, and vocalized cues such as "uh-huh," "I see," or "yes" are all positive attending behaviors. A pleasant tone of voice, gentle touching, and concern for the other person's comfort are other attending behaviors. Effective empathic or relational listeners give the other person their full attention.

> **INSIGHT**
>
> *When you give somebody your full attention and listen to them completely, you hear more than just their words; you discover their feelings and emotions and you get inside their soul.*
>
> Ann Henry Kline

Supporting

Many responses have a negative or nonsupportive effect; for example, interrupting the speaker, changing the subject, turning the conversation toward yourself, and otherwise demonstrating a lack of concern for the other person. Giving advice, attempting to manipulate the conversation, or indicating that you consider yourself superior are other behaviors that will have an adverse effect on the relationship. Sometimes the best response is silence. The speaker may need a "sounding board," not a "resounding board." Wise relational listeners know when to talk and when to just listen—and they generally listen more than they talk.

> **INSIGHT**
>
> *Did you ever stop to think that the words* listen *and* silent *use the same letters? That should tell us something.*

Empathizing

What is empathy? It is not sympathy, which is a feeling of compassion for another. Empathy is feeling and thinking *with* another person. The caring, empathic listener is able to go into the world of another—to see as the other sees, hear as the other hears, and feel as the other feels. Obviously, the person who has had more experience and lived longer stands a better chance of being an effective empathic listener. The person who has never been divorced, lost a child, been bankrupt, or lost a job may have a more difficult time relating to people with these problems than one who has experienced such things. But empathic behavior can be learned.

INSIGHT	*Listen and attend with the ears of your heart.*
	Saint Benedict

First, you must learn as much as you can about the other person. Second, you must accept the other person, even if you can't accept some aspects of that person's behavior. Third and most important, you must care enough to really listen—you must want to be an empathic listener. Read the boxed example of empathic and nonempathic listening on the following page.

It is obvious that Ted's fourth friend showed more empathy and was a more skilled relational listener. His words and actions demonstrated an ability to put himself in Ted's place. He showed that he felt Ted's pain and cared about him. We demonstrate empathy and understanding of others with noncommittal acknowledgment, brief expressions such as "Uh-huh," "I see," "Hum," or "Right." We should avoid such stock phrases as "Oh, it's not that bad," "You'll feel better tomorrow," "You're making too much of it," or "I know just how you feel." The truth is that no one knows exactly how someone else feels, and such trite phrases do little to help. They may even hurt because they tend to discount the other person's feelings.

APPRECIATIVE LISTENING

Appreciative listening means listening for enjoyment, whether you are listening to music, a speaker, theater, television, radio, or a film. It is the response of the listener, not the source of the message, that defines appreciative listening. Appreciative listening is subjective. For example, hard-rock music is not a source of appreciative listening for me. I would rather listen to Southern gospel or "golden oldies." My children and grandchildren would no doubt choose jazz, classical, contemporary, or country. You name it, and somebody in my family probably likes it. What we appreciate depends in large part on three factors: presentation, perception, and previous experience.

Four Friends: Which One Was the Empathic Listener?

Ted has left a good-paying job at the factory and is now a full-time student. It isn't easy with two kids. He and his wife, Bonnie, are scraping along, living off the meager salary she makes as a secretary. Neither of their families is in a position to offer any financial help, so things are tight.

Then the bottom seems to drop out. Bonnie discovers a suspicious lump and is scheduled to have it removed early the next week. An old football injury that Ted received in high school flares up and Ted's knee is painful. To top it off, both kids need new shoes, and Ted has just flunked a big chemistry test.

One night Bonnie takes the kids to visit a friend so that Ted can hit the books, and so she won't have to hear him complain. A friend of Ted's who knows of his trouble stops by to visit him. After listening to Ted's tale of woe, he says, "Yep, I know just how you feel. I really can sympathize with you. But after all into each life a little rain must fall. Just hang in there. Things will get better."

A short while after he leaves another friend comes by. After he listens to Ted a little while he says, "Grow up, Ted. Take it like a man. Your problems are not any worse than anyone else's."

Later a third friend comes by. After listening to Ted's story he says, "Well I've got to get going. If you need anything, just give me a call, old buddy."

Finally, a fourth friend comes by. He doesn't say much; he just listens, nods, and says a few "uh-huhs." Before the friend leaves, he says. "Ted, I just want you to know that I care about you and I hurt for you." The next day he sends an e-mail that says, "Just wanted to let you know that I am thinking about you." For the next few weeks, he checks in with Ted until the crisis passes.

Presentation

I just mentioned that I prefer gospel music to hard rock. But I don't enjoy *all* gospel. For example, I don't enjoy gospel music when it is presented in a "glitzy" setting, or when it is performed by someone who fails to demonstrate an understanding of the music's meaning. (I might add that I don't usually enjoy gospel when it is off-key or poorly done, but there are exceptions, such as the time I heard a 103-year-old man sing "Amazing Grace." Never have I enjoyed it more!) I enjoy hearing speakers who have expertise in a particular subject. Presentation encompasses many factors, such as the medium, the setting, and the style and personality of the presenter, to name just a few.

Perception

Sometimes it is our perception of the presentation, rather than the actual presentation, that most influences our listening pleasure or displeasure. Perception is an important factor in appreciative listening. For years, I did not care to listen to jazz music. Then I traveled with a boss who enjoyed jazz. While we were traveling I attended some jazz concerts with him and, as a result, developed an appreciation and taste for jazz music. And I still like it. Expectations play a large role in perception. If I attend a concert under duress with no expectation of enjoying the music (perhaps my wife insists that I attend, or my position in the community makes it the thing to do), I may be pleasantly surprised. However, I stand a better chance of enjoying the concert if I *expect* to enjoy it.

INSIGHT	*Perception is reality.*

Previous Experience

The discussion of perception makes it clear that previous experience influences what we enjoy listening to. In some cases, we enjoy listening to what we already know a lot about. Sometimes, however, expertise or previous experience prevents us from enjoying a presentation because we are too sensitive to imperfections. Some people enjoy the sounds of city traffic. Perhaps they grew up in a large city. The blare of horns honking, the sound of roaring engines accelerating, even the shrill shriek of sirens piercing the air—all these may remind them of a happy childhood. They appreciate hearing these sounds. Others, having grown up on a farm or in a small town, have learned to enjoy the sounds of nature. For them, a walk in the country provides sounds of enjoyment: the rustling of leaves in the breeze, the song of a robin, the babble of a brook.

Usually, if we associate a sound or other experience with pleasant memories, we appreciate or enjoy it. However, if the sound or experience is associated with unpleasant memories, we probably will not appreciate or enjoy it. But we can change. I did not enjoy jazz music when I first heard it, but now I do. We should keep our minds open to new experiences so that we can learn to be better appreciative listeners.

CRITICAL LISTENING

The ability to listen critically is essential in a democracy. On the job, in the community, at service clubs, in places of worship, in the family—there is practically no place you can go where critical listening is unimportant. Politicians; the media; salespeople; advocates of policies and procedures; and our own financial, emotional, intellectual, physical, and spiritual needs require us to place a premium on critical listening and reasoning.

There are three aspects to critical listening. Aristotle, the classical Greek rhetorician, outlined these three factors more than 2,000 years ago in his treatise *The Rhetoric*. They are as follows: *ethos*, or speaker credibility; *logos*, or logical arguments; and *pathos*, or emotional appeals.

Ethos

The two most critical indicators of speaker credibility are expertness and trustworthiness. A speaker may be expert or competent and still not be trustworthy. For example, an autocratic dictator of a third-world country might be an expert on the question of his country's possession of nuclear arms, but I would not trust his opinion. On the other hand, a person might be trustworthy but not an expert on the subject. I trust my best friend; he would tell me the truth about nuclear arms in that third-world country, if he knew and I asked him. But his information would be of questionable validity because he is simply not an expert on that country.

When listening to a message that requires a critical judgment or response, ask yourself, "Is the speaker a credible source, one who is both an expert on the subject and who can be trusted to be honest, unbiased, and straightforward?" Remember that friendliness and charisma do not take the place of credibility. A person may be an expert in one area but ill informed in another. Effective critical listening requires careful judgment about the expertness and trustworthiness of the speaker. In fact, ethos may be the single most important factor in critical listening and thinking. However, credibility (ethos) without substance (logos) is not enough.

Logos

Even speakers with high ethos often make errors in reasoning or logic, not by intention, but by accident, carelessness, inattention to detail, or lack of analysis. Critical listeners have a right to expect well-supported arguments from speakers, arguments that contain both true propositions and valid inferences or conclusions.

Assessing the logos or logical element
    a. Are the data true?
    b. What is the source of the data?
    c. Are the data the best that can be obtained?
    d. Are the data accurately portrayed?
    e. Does the speaker's conclusion follow from the data?
    f. Is the conclusion a certainty, or are exceptions possible?

Both ethos and logos are crucial elements of critical listening, but reliance on just these two elements without consideration of pathos would be akin to attempting to sit on a three-legged stool with one leg missing. Pathos is the third leg.

Pathos

The psychological or emotional element of communication is often misunderstood and misused. Speakers often use psychological appeals to gain an emotional response from listeners. Effective critical listeners carefully determine the focus of the speaker's message. Speakers may appeal to one or more needs, desires, or values that are important to us, including adventure, thrift, curiosity, fear, creativity, companionship, guilt, independence, loyalty, power, pride, sympathy, and altruism. There are many others, of course; the list is a long one.

Assessing the pathos or emotional element

   a. Is the speaker attempting to manipulate rather than persuade me?
   b. What is the speaker's intent?
   c. Is the speaker combining logos with pathos?
   d. Am I responding merely to the pathos?
   e. Next week or next year will I be satisfied with the decision I am making today based on my response to this speaker?

Effective critical listening depends on the listener analyzing all three elements of the message: ethos, or speaker credibility; logos, or logical argument; and pathos, or emotional appeal.

DISCRIMINATIVE LISTENING

Discriminative listening is the foundation for the other four types of listening. Being sensitive to changes in the speaker's rate, volume, force, pitch, and emphasis enhances informative listening. Using supportive phrases such as "uh-huh" or "I see" can strengthen relational listening. Being able to detect differences among instruments in an orchestra or parts sung by an a cappella vocal group enhances appreciative listening. Finally, sensitivity to pauses and other verbal and nonverbal cues allows those engaging in critical listening to more accurately judge not only the speaker's message, but his intentions as well. Obviously, many people have good discriminatory listening ability in some areas but not in others. However, it is difficult, if not impossible, to be an effective informative, relational, appreciative, or critical listener without possessing at least some skill as a discriminative listener. Of course, one may be effective in the other types of listening and not be a good discriminative listener in every situation, as the boxed example on the following page demonstrates.

"Oh, I Had No Idea"

Nanette is an exceptional counselor, always very adept at picking up minute variations in a person's voice that might signal a shift in feelings. She has a gift for applying what she hears to relational listening. However, she has almost no ability to discriminate among the different sounds that come from an automobile engine.

One evening she pulls into the driveway, her fan belt squealing. Her husband says, "Nanette, can't you hear that sound? Don't you know what it means? You're wearing out a belt."

"Oh," Nanette replies. "I thought I heard something, but I guess I just sorta tuned it out. Is it something serious?"

"You bet it is," says her husband. "You're lucky you got home. If the belt had broken, the car would have overheated, and you would have stalled."

"Oh," Nanette says, "I had no idea."

Nanette possesses great discriminative listening skills in one area of her life—counseling—but she does not have the ability to discriminate when it comes to sounds coming from her car.

Three factors influence discriminative listening: hearing ability, awareness of sound structure, and integration of nonverbal cues.

Hearing Ability

Obviously, people who lack the ability to hear well will have difficulty in discriminating among sounds. Often this problem is more acute for some frequencies, or pitches, than others. People may have a high-frequency hearing loss, often from prolonged exposure to noise, while retaining normal or near normal hearing for low frequencies. Such people may experience little difficulty discriminating among the lower-pitched vowel sounds, but significant difficulty discriminating among higher-pitched consonant sounds. For instance, they may have problems discriminating among the words *thin*, *fin*, *tin*, and *sin*. They would hear the *in* part of each word clearly but have difficulty distinguishing the weak high-pitched sounds at the beginning of each word, resulting in potentially significant misunderstanding of a message.

Awareness of Sound Structure

Native speakers become quite proficient at recognizing vowel and consonant sounds at the beginning, middle, or end of words. For example, a listener might hear *this sandal* when what the speaker said was *this handle*, but because English words do not begin with *sb*, they would not hear *this sbean* for *this bean*.

Integration of Nonverbal Cues

Nonverbal cues include more than gestures, head nods, and such. The way words are emphasized and pronounced also sends nonverbal messages. The words themselves don't always communicate true feeling; the words the speaker chooses to stress and the gestures the speaker uses may be the key to understanding the true or intended meaning.

Effective listening, whether informative, relational, appreciative, critical, or discriminative, requires skill. The next chapter presents 18 instructions that will help you be a better listener. As you read these instructions, think about which ones will work best with each of the types of listening we just discussed. First, you may want to find out how good you are at the five types of listening.

Exercise	How Good Are You at Various Types of Listening?

1. What type of listening is easiest for you? Why?
2. What type of listening is most difficult? Why?
3. What types of listening seem to be the most difficult for most people? For your peers? Parents? Bosses and supervisors?
4. What type or types of listening are you going to target for your own self-improvement? Why?
5. What will be the benefits of improvement?
6. What specifically are you going to do to improve? If this is tough to answer, think back on the information given in previous chapters, especially the bad habits of listening discussed in Chapter 3 and the barriers to listening discussed in Chapter 4. Also, the instructions for listening presented in Chapter 6 should help you.

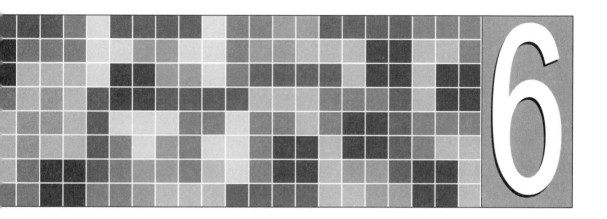

Instructions for Listening

Objective: Apply the 18 instructions to become a better listener in all situations.

Tasks: Explain the 6 instructions for how to think about listening.

Explain the 6 instructions for how to feel about listening.

Explain the 6 instructions for what to do about listening.

Describe how you will apply these instructions to your own listening behavior.

We have looked at the need for good listening, false assumptions about listening, barriers to listening, the listening process, and types of listening. By now you should have learned some new techniques that can make you a more effective listener on the job, in school, and with your family and friends. Now it is time to focus attention directly on 18 instructions for effective listening.

These instructions have been taught to many different kinds of people, including college students, military personnel, managers, and workers in small businesses and Fortune 500 companies. They have been tested, and they have stood the test. People who have followed these instructions have become significantly better listeners. These instructions are divided into three groups: (1) what you *think* about listening, (2) what you *feel* about listening, and (3) what you *do* about listening. You may be tempted to look ahead to the instructions on what you do about listening, but all 18 are important. What you think and what you feel will influence what you do.

WHAT YOU <u>THINK</u> ABOUT LISTENING

Although thinking, feeling, and doing go hand in hand, thinking is the best place to begin. After all, effective listening takes effort—it requires maximum thinking power. Here are six instructions to improve how you think about listening.

Understand the Complexities of Listening

Most of us take good listening for granted, so we don't work very hard at improving. Listening is a complex activity, as I have emphasized throughout this book. Knowing the fallacies about listening can keep you from being trapped by them. Recognizing bad listening habits keeps you from falling into them. Realizing that the process involves more than just receiving messages will help you focus on the other components as well. Recognizing the five major types of listening will help you to consciously direct your energies appropriately.

Listening requires an active response. Effective listening doesn't just happen; it takes thought—and thinking can be hard work.

INSIGHT	*Effective listening doesn't just happen; it takes thought and hard work.*

Prepare to Listen

Preparation consists of three phases—long term, mid term, and short term. As I have said before, becoming an effective listener is a lifetime endeavor.

You can do two things to improve your listening skills for the long term. First, practice listening to difficult material. Too many people do not challenge their listening abilities. Because many radio and television programs do not require concentrated or careful listening, your listening skills seldom improve through repeated exposure to broadcast media. You have to stretch if you want to grow, so force yourself to listen carefully to congressional debates, news programs, lectures, sermons, or other complex material that requires concentration. Second, build your vocabulary. Improving your vocabulary will improve your conversation skills and reading skills as well as your listening skills. The more words you learn, the better listener you will become. Long-term improvement of your listening skills takes discipline, but it is worth it.

INSIGHT	*Life is tons of discipline. Your first discipline is your vocabulary. . . . And your delight is in that power.*
	Robert Frost

Mid-term preparation requires that you do background research before you begin listening. If you are a student, read the assigned material before the lecture; you will be in a much better position to understand and learn from what the instructor says in class. If you find yourself in a time crunch, even skimming the reading material before the lecture will help.

On the job, reading background material or taking an advance look at slides or charts will prepare you to listen. You will get more out of the briefing and so be able to discuss the presentation knowledgeably with your boss and colleagues. You'll receive payoff both personally and professionally when you are prepared.

Short-term preparation may be described as an immediate readiness to listen. When the speaker's mouth opens, you should open your ears. That is not the time to hunt for a pen, read a letter from home, or think about some unrelated subject. Good listeners—really good listeners—are in a spring-loaded position, ready to listen. It is important to *prepare* to listen. Sometimes the first words spoken are the most important. They may set the tone for what is to follow, or they may provide the key for how to listen to the rest of the message.

Read the following exercise. If you had trouble answering the bus question, analyze why you had trouble. If you did not, decide why it was not a problem. After you have familiarized yourself with the exercise, read it to someone else, taking care to pause between each sentence long enough for the listener to comprehend what you are saying. After you have read the message to others and they have answered the question, discuss why they answered the way they did.

---

cise   The Bus Question

driving a bus that is leaving Nashville. Your destination is Atlanta. When you start, there are 30 ngers. At the first stop, 10 people get off and 9 people get on. At the second stop, 2 people get d 2 people get on. At the third stop, 12 people get on and 16 people get off. At the fourth stop, ple get on and 3 people get off.

low, what color are the bus driver's eyes? (The answer is on page 58.)

Adjust to the Situation

No two listening situations are exactly the same. The time and place, the speaker, and the message all change. Many other less obvious variables also affect listening. Physiological variables such as rest, hunger, comfort, endurance; psychological variables such as emotional stability, rapport with the speaker, knowledge of the subject; and physical factors such as the size and appearance of the room may all affect listening. Obviously, some variables will have a positive effect on listening while others will have a negative effect. For example, a speaker's accent and poor grammar or a room with poor acoustics could present barriers to effective listening. Be aware of possible barriers and think of strategies to help you adjust to the situation.

Consider habits four through seven discussed in Chapter 3. When listeners are preoccupied, listen for what they expect rather than what is actually said, or are influenced by prejudice and stereotypes, they demonstrate an inability to adjust to dynamic situations. They are locked into their old thinking and they tend to disregard or misunderstand what is said.

Answer to the Bus Question

To correctly answer the problem, the listener must listen as soon as the speaker begins talking. The answer is found in the first word of the first sentence. You, the listener, are driving the bus, so the color of the bus driver's eyes is, of course, the color of your eyes. By the way, the majority of people don't answer correctly when the question is read to them.

INSIGHT   *You can't step into the same stream twice.*

Heraclitus

Focus on Ideas or Key Points

You understand the process, you have prepared well, and you adjust to the situation—yet at times you fail as a listener. You fail because you didn't listen to the right things. For example, you may remember a funny story the speaker told to make a point, but you missed the point. The Bus Question was tricky because listeners tend to focus so much on the numbers of people getting on and off the bus that they forget they are the bus driver.

As Sergeant Joe Friday of *Dragnet* would say, "Just the facts ma'am." Certainly there are situations where the facts are all that matter, but this is not usually the case. Some people boast, "I listen only for the facts." The trouble is that concentrating exclusively on individual facts can cause you to miss the main ideas. Facts A, B, and C may be interesting in their own right, but the speaker's reason for offering them is usually to develop a generalization from them. Generalizations, not facts, are often most important.

Capitalize on the Speed Differential

Thought can operate much faster than speech. An average person may speak two or three words a second—120 to 180 words a minute. In bursts of enthusiasm, we may even speak a little faster. Most public speakers speak somewhat

Listening: Rote Memory vs. Key Ideas

In studies conducted some years ago at the University of New Mexico, I discovered that students who did best on all but rote memory examinations were those who listened for key points and ideas. Interestingly, those who attempted to memorize minute details did only slightly better on low-level rote memory exams than the individuals who focused on ideas—and they did much worse when long-term retention was the criterion. Although there are times when memorization is necessary, such as when listening to directions or memorizing a mathematical formula, it is usually best to focus on ideas or key points.

slower, especially to large audiences. Yet most listeners can process up to 500 words per minute, depending on the nature and difficulty of the material.

Special machines can compress speech on tape, while removing the distortions normally associated with fast forwarding a tape or playing a tape at a faster speed. Compression is accomplished through systematic removal of segments so small that listeners do not notice distortion. Experiments in which listening time is cut in half reveal little significant loss in learning. Admittedly, listeners are ready for a break after such intensive listening. Effective listening requires hard thinking, especially if the material is challenging.

The results of these experiments point to the possibility of capitalizing on the speed differential. Unfortunately, the differential between speed of thought and speed of speech promotes daydreaming or distraction. This is not the case with good listeners, however. They use the time differential to good advantage. They focus on what the speaker says and its importance to them as listeners. They avoid the bad habits of listening discussed earlier. Skilled listeners capitalize on the speed differential by using the time wisely. This may explain why top listeners—colonels and lieutenant colonels attending the United States Air Force's Air War College—recently reported that they learned more from lectures than from any other method of instruction. They have learned to capitalize on the speed differential.

Search for Relationships Between What the Speaker Is Saying and What You Already Know

Think how much easier it is to listen to information—even new information—about a subject you already are familiar with than it is to listen and retain information on a new or unfamiliar subject. Speakers can enhance listening by adapting to their audience and presenting the material so that it relates to their current knowledge. You as a listener can take what the speaker is saying and relate it to knowledge you already have.

Seeking relationships between the new material and what you already know requires concentrated thinking. It is easier to simply tune out. There was a time in my early college years when I could not see the relevance of some required classes to my course of study. A professor for whom I had great respect explained to me, "John, someday you will come to understand that all information is part of a large mosaic or universe of knowledge. When that happens, you will value all learning. Always look for how the information relates to what you already know and what you need to know, and you will always find something." He was right.

The next exercise consists of two lists. If you read them to yourself, make sure you follow the directions. Read the first list once; then look away and see how many you can remember. Then do the same with the other list. If you are in a class, you can make your own lists—the first without meaning, the second with meaning and pattern. This activity will help you understand the importance of looking for relationships between what the speaker is saying and what you already know.

Exercise	Remembering

Say the following 10 "words" out loud one time. *Then look away and see how many you can remember.*

mip	bril	frot	wup	des
ner	sten	lak	zop	sim

How did you do? Unless you are highly unusual in your ability to use rote memory, you probably did not do very well, for the list consisted of nonsense syllables. Now, try the next exercise and see how you do.

Exercise	Remembering: Another Try

Say these words out loud one time, *reading down the first column and then down the second column. Then look away and see how many you can remember.*

Boston	Houston
New York	Dallas
Philadelphia	Phoenix
Atlanta	Los Angeles
New Orleans	San Francisco

Did you do better on the second list? Chances are that you could remember almost all of them. The reason? The words mean something to you—they are the names of well-known cities in the United States. You may have visited some of them. You probably know something about all of them. Perhaps you pictured landmarks in each city. If you are a sports fan, you may have thought about the professional teams that play there. Your memory may have been aided by the fact that the names are ordered somewhat geographically starting in the northeastern part of the United States and moving south and west. The point is this: When we see relationships between the message and what we already know, we can listen better, remember better, and learn more. Look for relationships between what the speaker is saying and what you already know.

WHAT YOU <u>FEEL</u> ABOUT LISTENING

We began by discussing what you think about listening because effective listening requires rigorous thought. But possession of the sharpest mind will not make you a good listener if your feelings hinder you. The following six sections contain instructions for improving your "feel" for listening.

Want to Listen

Wanting to listen is basic—you must intend to listen. We can all recall having been forced to listen to something that we didn't really want to listen to. Listening under duress seldom results in understanding or enjoyment, although there are exceptions. You may have attended a meeting or a social event out of a sense of duty, yet found it profitable. The reason? You decided to make the best of the situation; you made up your mind to listen.

Sometimes you know you don't want to listen. At other times, you may be unaware that you don't want to listen. And at still other times, your actions may indicate that you don't want to listen when you really do. All three of these situations involve your feelings about listening. The first two reflect your true feelings. The third affects the speaker's perception of your feelings.

It is difficult—indeed, nearly impossible—to really listen if you don't want to. It also helps if the person speaking believes that you want to listen.

Delay Judgment

There are times when you must be a critical or judgmental listener. Chapter 5 discussed critical listening. Sometimes you must weigh the merits of what the speaker is saying and make crucial decisions based on what you hear. There are also times when you must judge the speaker, as in job interviews, campaign speeches, and debates. The problem is that you may judge the speaker instead of the content, or you may form judgments before the speaker has finished.

Supervisors often wonder why people in their organizations won't level with them. They need only to consider the messenger in ancient Rome who paid with his life for bringing bad news. An ancient Turkish proverb says, "The

Exercise   Are You Listening?

Margo has been in a mid-level management position for about a year. She has responsibility for sixty people in her unit who report to her through four department heads. Margo goes out of her way to talk to all the employees, but she especially makes time for the four department heads. She lets them know that she cares about them as individuals and as colleagues. One afternoon Jill, the head of the marketing department, asks if she can talk with Margo about a personal problem.

Because Margo is going to be out of the office for a few days, she is hurrying to finish a project, but she tells Jill to come into her office. While Jill is talking, Margo begins to fidget. Although she tries to appear interested in what Jill is saying, Margo is not giving Jill her full attention.

Jill stops in the middle of a sentence and says, "Are you listening? I don't think you are with me. I'll talk to you when you get back, if you have time." Margo protests that she is listening, but her actions communicated something else.

Jill leaves the office. Margo sits there upset that she had not been a good listener when one of her best subordinates needed her.

Questions
1. What should Margo have said or done when Jill asked to talk with her?
2. What should Margo do now?
3. How do you think Jill felt? Will Margo's behavior affect her relationship with Jill? Will it affect her relationship with others in the office?
4. What other observations do you have?

messenger with bad news should keep one foot in the stirrup." Delaying judgment and judging the content rather than the speaker will lead to better listening and more honest communication.

Admit Your Biases

We all have likes and dislikes. This is natural and to be expected. The problem comes when we let our biases get in the way of understanding the speaker's message. For example, suppose you have had three bad experiences with people from Chicago and you learn that the speaker you have come to hear is from Chicago. You may immediately distrust him or discredit what he has to say. Only by admitting your prejudice against people from Chicago will you be able to think beyond your past experiences and listen effectively to what this speaker has to say.

Before you reject the above example as irrelevant, consider a time when you got sick after eating a certain food. You knew a virus and not the food caused the sickness, but it was quite a while before that food again tasted good to you. In a

I Am Proud of You Because You Were Honest

A boy who was one month shy of getting a driver's license decided to confess to his father that he had driven the family car the previous night. His younger sister's promised ride to gymnastics class hadn't arrived, and it was the night of her final rehearsal before a performance. He made the decision to take her even though he did not yet have a driver's license. He was sure that he hadn't been seen and would never be found out. Still, his conscience was bothering him, and his family had always stressed honesty and openness. He decided to tell his father.

His father was furious. He scarcely heard the reason, and he failed to consider that the boy had taken it upon himself to confess. He told the boy that the act would delay his getting a driver's license by six months. Later, the father rethought the situation and said, "Son, I acted hastily. My emotions got the best of me. You were wrong to drive the car because you broke the law. But, frankly, I am proud of you. You took your sister to her important gymnastics rehearsal. More than that, I am proud that you were honest about it."

Although the boy had done wrong, the father also made a mistake in not delaying judgment until he had heard the explanation. Fortunately, he had second thoughts and later made a more rational judgment.

similar way, biases from past experiences, can influence what you hear and the meaning you derive from it. If you want to be an effective listener, you must know and admit your biases.

Don't Tune Out Dry Subjects

Whenever you are tempted to tune out something because you think it will be boring or useless, remember that you cannot evaluate the importance of the message until you have heard it. By then the opportunity to listen effectively will have passed. As was stated earlier, you must *intend* to listen.

How to stay focused when the subject is dry
   a. Put yourself in the speaker's place. Try to see the speaker's point of view, and try to understand the speaker's attitude toward the subject.
   b. Review frequently what the speaker has said. Try to summarize the message as the speaker would summarize it.
   c. Constantly ask yourself positive questions about what the speaker is saying: How can I use this information? How can I share this information with others? What else could be said about this subject?
   d. Ask yourself, "What does the speaker know that I don't?"

e. Find at least one major application or conclusion from every message you hear. Ask, "What's in this message for me?" Then find the answer.

f. Listen as though you are going to be required to present the same message to a different audience later.

Effective listeners have discovered the value of listening to messages they might have initially considered to be "dry." Sometimes the messages aren't so dry after all. Even when they are, there still may be something of value in them.

Accept Responsibility for Understanding

Don't assume this attitude: "Here I am! Teach me—if you can." Such listeners believe knowledge can be poured into them like water is poured into a jug. They believe the responsibility rests with the one doing the pouring; that is, they believe it is the speaker's fault if effective listening does not occur.

Admittedly, the speaker bears a large responsibility for how well the audience listens. Clear organization, engaging support materials, and appropriate delivery do in fact aid listening. However, good listeners accept the responsibility for listening and understanding.

Exercise	Listening Triads: An Exercise in Understanding

Form groups of three people. The people in each triad should face each other and be far enough from other triads to carry on a conversation. Each triad decides on a topic for discussion such as a current event. It must be a subject that all three participants want to discuss. Let participants in each triad designate themselves as Wolf, Bear, and Lion.

Wolf begins the conversation on the selected subject with Bear. Before Bear can respond to Wolf, Bear must summarize what Wolf has said. Then Bear can speak. After Bear has finished, Wolf must summarize what Bear has said. The conversation continues this way for 5 to 10 minutes. All this time Lion must keep silent except to intercede if either Wolf or Bear do not follow the rules or do an inaccurate job of summarizing what the other person has said.

After 5 to 10 minutes, change roles. Bear initiates a conversation with Lion; Wolf keeps silent except to intercede if necessary. After another 5 to 10 minutes switch roles again. This time Lion initiates a conversation with Wolf. Bear keeps silent unless intercession is necessary.

Questions

After the three sessions are finished, each triad answers the following questions:

1. Did you have difficulty listening to the other person?
2. Did you have difficulty formulating what to say and also listening?
3. Was it difficult not to participate in the conversation when you were in the intercessory role?

4. What would it be like if you always had to summarize before you could speak? In what ways would it help communication and listening? In what ways would it be a hindrance?

Share with the Class

If you are in a class, select one person to share your triad's answers with the rest of the class.

Encourage Others to Talk

It doesn't seem as if most people need much encouragement to talk. In fact, at times we hate to give them too much encouragement for fear they will talk longer. However, in small groups or one-on-one settings, you may find you need to encourage others to talk. After all, you can't listen if no one is talking. Besides, the most popular people in the world are the ones who get others to talk.

How to encourage others to talk
   a. Stop talking. You can't listen if you're talking.
   b. Give positive feedback. Look and act interested. Nods, alertness, and smiles encourage the other person.
   c. Ask questions that show interest and attention.
   d. Empathize with the other person. Put yourself in his or her place.
   e. Keep confidences. If the information is sensitive, don't share it with others.
   f. Share information with them. We tend to talk to those who talk to us. So if you want other people to share information with you, share information with them.
   g. Make a conscious effort to talk less than the other person.

WHAT YOU <u>DO</u> ABOUT LISTENING

What we think about listening and what we feel about listening are both fundamental to skillful listening, but the skills themselves are crucial. Skills form the "doing" element of listening. The following sections present six positive actions you can take to improve your listening behavior.

Establish Eye Contact with the Speaker

Listening has a positive relationship with eye contact. First, the better eye contact you have with the speaker, the better you will listen. Second, better eye contact with the speaker encourages the speaker to communicate better. It is easier to talk to an audience that demonstrates through effective eye contact that it is paying attention.

Eye contact is vitally important in relational listening, where you are seeking not only to understand the message but also to understand the person.

Exercise   Effect of Listener Eye Contact on the Speaker

These two experiments will demonstrate the effect of eye contact on the speaker.

Experiment 1

This one is simple. While the speaker is talking, instruct listeners to look out the window or at the ceiling. Even the most disciplined speaker will have trouble continuing. If she continues, her presentation will suffer.

Experiment 2

This one takes more in-depth participation from audience members. Without the speaker's knowledge, instruct each audience member to look just a few inches to the right (their right, the speaker's left) of the speaker. After some time, the speaker will unconsciously shift position slightly to the left to align herself with where the audience is looking. Give the speaker a minute or two to get comfortable in that position; then have audience members shift their eye contact to the right of the speaker. An audience can cause the speaker to move just through their eye contact. It is important that all audience members shift their gaze in the same direction and that the shift be subtle. The speaker must not know that they are attempting to use eye contact to manipulate her.

Effective eye contact communicates to the other person that you are making an earnest attempt to listen.

Eye contact aids listening of all types: relational, informative, appreciative, critical, and discriminative listening. In fact, eye contact is perhaps one of the most important determinants of good listening. It can help the speaker, and it almost always helps the listener.

INSIGHT   *The wise man listens with his eyes as well as with his ears.*

Ancient Proverb

Of course, not all eye contact is of equal value. To achieve the kind of eye contact that helps you listen better, you must do more than simply look in the direction of the person speaking. Simply staring at or "through" a speaker is not the kind of eye contact that will aid your listening or encourage the speaker.

You give effective eye contact to someone you like, to someone who is very special or important to you, or to someone who is saying something of vital interest to you. Watch an audience that is listening to a very entertaining, engaging, first-rate speaker—one who has their complete attention. Take special note of their eye contact with the speaker. You will see positive eye contact that aids the listener and the speaker.

How to establish positive eye contact with the speaker

    a. In one-on-one or small-group settings, sit or stand where you can look directly at the person speaking.

    b. In large groups, sit in the front and center of the audience. You can more easily establish eye contact with the speaker from this vantage point.

    c. Don't get so involved in taking notes that you fail to look often at the speaker. The speaker's gestures, movements, and facial expression are often an important part of the message.

    d. Don't allow yourself to be distracted by the setting or other people. Focus on the speaker and the message.

    e. Don't look at others who enter or leave while the speaker is talking. This practice not only interrupts your train of thought—it adds to the distraction of the speaker.

    f. Speakers sometimes exhibit a visual aid too soon or neglect to remove it when they have finished using it. Focus on the visual aid only when it is relevant to the point being discussed.

    g. Never sleep when someone is talking to you! This may seem self-evident, but let's face it—in the busyness of our lives, we tend to become passive whenever we listen. Passivity encourages reduced attention, which leads to drowsiness. It is better to stand up, or even leave the room, rather than fall asleep.

Take Notes Effectively

Some people recommend not taking notes so you can focus your attention wholly on what the speaker is saying. This practice works well for listeners who are blessed with a great memory; most of us aren't. Taking notes will not only help you remember; it will help you organize what the speaker is saying. It may even aid your understanding and retention—after all, effective note taking will require you to think.

He listens well who takes notes.   **INSIGHT**

Dante Alighieri

There are many ways to take notes. You can use linear outlining—the type of outlining that most of us learned as children—or "mind mapping," in which the main concept is placed in the middle of the page with lines radiating out to subordinate concepts. Ask different people what techniques they use. Try a few different methods and find what works best for you.

This may sound far-fetched, but I often take notes in poetic form. The poetry isn't all that good, but the technique forces me to think deeply about the meaning I want to capture. The process keeps me awake when my body is telling me it would like to sleep. For example, I recently attended a Troy State University graduation that was held at its Montgomery, Alabama, campus. The ceremony was held at night. I had worked all day, had eaten too much for dinner, and wanted to stay awake. Beyond that, I wanted to be an effective listener. I especially wanted to hear what Chancellor Jack Hawkins, Jr. (my boss) and the commencement speaker, Mr. William C. Taylor (president and CEO of Mercedes-Benz U.S. International, Inc.) said. I resorted to poetry to capture Dr. Hawkins's four points, which were to be good citizens, be supportive alumni, return to the campus often, and send other people to Troy State University to get degrees. I wanted to capture Mr. Taylor's emphasis on continual improvement, communication, lifelong learning, and teamwork:

> President Martindale told about the class
> And welcomed Chancellor Hawkins to the stand
> At the end of his positive message
> He received a well-deserved hand
>
> He challenged graduates to be good citizens
> Said supportive alumni they should be
> They should visit the campus often
> And send others to get a degree
>
> Then Mr. William Taylor
> Gave the commencement speech
> He told graduates to never be satisfied
> But continue to stretch and reach
>
> All should continuously improve
> They must effectively communicate
> Have the ability and desire to learn
> Be a team and participate

Admittedly, this is not great poetry, but it worked as an effective note-taking device for me. Find what works for you. Don't be bound by the way other people take notes.

One of the most effective and popular note-taking techniques is the Cornell system. You might find that this system works for you, or you may find that you can adapt it to your needs. This system, created nearly 50 years ago by Walter Pauk at Cornell University,* is sometimes called the T-note system because its three sections are divided by an upside down "T" drawn on ordinary

---

*Walter Pauk, *How to Study in College*, 7th ed. Boston: Houghton Mifflin (2001), pp. 236–241.

| Figure 6.1 | Cornell note-taking system. |

How to Remember

Why does memory fail?
— 2 types — long vs. short
—short-term — use immediately
—long-term — needed mins, hrs, days later

Memory like a muscle
— Must exercise memory
—like a muscle — use or lose
—use → stronger; not use → weaker

What are five techniques of memory?
— Five memory techniques
1. Repetition — recite over and over
—grocery list, part in play

2. Chunking — into chunks/categories
—divide list — canned goods, produce, paper

3. Patterning — logical arrangement
—e.g. Attention (selectivity, strength, sustain)

4. Association — w/something else
—padlock combination
—names: Adam Johnson/John Adams

5. Visualization
—slides/vis-aids/can create in mind

Must use memory to not lose it — both short-term and long-term. Techniques are Repetition, Chunking, Patterning, Association, and Visualization

notepaper. Figure 6.1 shows how a student used the Cornell system to take notes from a lecture on "How to Remember."

- Section 1 is the large section on the right. Take your notes here during the lecture or speech in an ordinary linear outline form or however is most comfortable for you.
- Section 2 is the narrow "cue column" to the left. Leave it blank as you listen. Later you will use it to highlight ideas, give examples, clarify meaning, or make a note of questions or key points that you want to focus on.
- Section 3, at the bottom of the page, is the summary or overview area where you will later briefly capture the essence of what is on the page.

Whatever note-taking method you use, keep this in mind. You took notes to help you later, for a test or for your job. When you need the notes you probably won't have a lot of time to spare. Make your notes useable.

Most of the 18 instructions for listening given at the end of this chapter (see page 74) apply to note taking as well because good note taking begins with good listening.

Tips for better notes

a. Take a few minutes before the presentation to get your brain in gear. Review notes from previous meetings and scan the background readings or other material that you have previously studied.

b. Think about what you expect to gain from the presentation.

c. Have pen and paper (or laptop) ready so you can take notes when the speaker begins.

d. Accept that your mind may wander; be ready to refocus.

e. Listen with your eyes as well as your ears. Watching speakers often reveals what they consider important. When speakers read from their notes or look carefully at them before speaking, it may signal that the information is especially important.

f. Listen for introductory, concluding, and transition words and phrases that reveal the structure of the presentation. Also listen for vocal emphasis. If the speaker repeats something, it is usually important.

g. Remember that if presenters write something down or present it using a visual aid, they usually consider it important.

h. Don't attempt to write everything down in your notes. As mentioned earlier, effective listeners focus on the key ideas or main points.

i. Write clearly enough that you can understand your writing later, or at least allow time to decipher your notes before they grow "cold." It's disheartening to review your notes two weeks later only to find that they make no sense.

j. Review your notes soon after the presentation. Consider editing them. If you use the Cornell system, fill in sections two and three. After 24 hours we forget half of what we heard. Some estimate that we lose 80 percent within a week.

k. Circle or highlight the most important points. Develop your own system of highlighting and underlining.

l. Don't rely on listening later to a tape of the speech. You may not have the time. Looking at your notes for a few minutes is generally sufficient and is much more time-efficient than listening to the entire speech again.

Be a Physically Involved Listener

Just what does being a physically involved listener mean? You have already seen that listening requires more than just hearing. You have also seen that making eye contact and taking notes will help to keep you from becoming passive. There are other physical actions you can take to aid listening.

How to stay physically involved in listening

    a. Use good posture. Sit up straight, yet comfortably. Good posture aids breathing and alertness. It also communicates positive interest to the speaker.

    b. Follow the speaker. If the speaker moves, turn your head or rotate in your chair to maintain eye contact and attention. This movement also helps you remain alert.

    c. Don't be deadpan. Facial expressions and head nods and tilts provide positive feedback to the speaker.

    d. Use your hands not only to take notes, but also to show approval by applause when appropriate.

    e. Participate when audience involvement is encouraged. Ask questions. Respond when a show of hands is called for. Be an active listener.

    f. Smile.

If you are reading this book as part of a class, decide that within the next few days each of you will observe the physical presence of people as they listen to a speaker. The best time to do this is when you don't have to listen closely to the speaker. Be assured that although you won't be learning as much from what the speaker says, you will learn much about people's physical involvement in the listening process. Note the listening behavior of different people. Do they demonstrate energy and enthusiasm as listeners? Discuss with the class what you observed and what you inferred about the listening of the audience or audiences you observed. Now be introspective and honest. What kind of physical listening behavior do you demonstrate? What can you do to be a more energetic and physically involved listener? What do you expect the results will be?

Avoid Negative Mannerisms

Everyone has mannerisms. Watch anyone for a period of time and you will be convinced of this. If your mannerisms do not cause a negative reaction, don't worry about them. If a mannerism is positive or encouraging and brings a positive response, make a mental note to do it more often. Unfortunately, some mannerisms are negative or distracting. These should be avoided, for they are not only a distraction to the speaker, they also distract other listeners. You will not be popular if you are a distracter. Furthermore, negative mannerisms often indicate misplaced energy—energy that could be directed toward listening.

Negative mannerisms to avoid

    a. Fidgeting, tapping a pencil, or playing with a rubber band or some other object. The effect on you may be neutral, but such actions distract other listeners and are an annoyance to the speaker.

b. Continually looking at the clock or your watch.

c. Reading a paper, balancing a checkbook, rearranging items in your wallet, or engaging in other behavior that takes focus away from the speaker.

d. Displaying arrogance, superiority, or lack of interest in the speaker and message.

e. Talking or passing notes to others in the audience.

In short, avoid any mannerism or behavior that detracts from the speaker or the message.

Exercise Your Listening Muscles

Listening takes practice. Just as an athlete must work out regularly and a musician must practice daily, so you must work consistently to be an effective listener. Practice the techniques discussed in this chapter and you will become a better listener. Practice may not make perfect, but as a wise man named Publius Syrus said two thousand years ago, "Practice is the best of all instructors."

INSIGHT	*Practice in time becomes second nature.*
	Plutarch

Exposure to challenging material and difficult listening situations will stretch your listening ability and build your listening muscles. If you knew that you would be required to carry a 50-pound weight 100 yards in less than a minute, you wouldn't practice by carrying a 30-pound weight. You would practice by carrying at least a 50-pound weight, and you probably would condition yourself to carry it more than 100 yards in less than a minute. With this kind of practice, you would be more than equal to the task. And so it is with listening: practice to *at least* the level you will be required to perform—perhaps a bit above.

Finally, stretch your vocabulary. Nothing will pay greater listening dividends. Learn the meanings of new words and acronyms. Listen to and read material that contains challenging words. Keep a dictionary nearby. Look up new words as you read them, or jot them down as you listen so you can look up the meanings later.

Follow the Golden Rule

Do unto others as you would have them do unto you. The central focus of all effective communication is "other directedness." There are exceptions to most other listening rules. For example, there are times when a listener shouldn't pre-pare; preparation may prevent openness to new ideas. There are times when the objective is not to focus on key points but to listen for subordinate ideas or sup-porting material. There are times when we should not delay judgment—we must act! Although these rules have exceptions, the Golden Rule does not. The effective listener is *always* other-directed, focused on the other person. Be the kind of listener you want others to be when you are talking. Ask, "How would I want others to listen to me?" That's how to listen.

Therefore, however you want people to treat you, so treat them, for this is the Law and the Prophets.	**INSIGHT**
Jesus, as recorded in Matthew 7:12 NASB	

Congratulations—you've almost finished the book. You've discovered the fallacies, bad habits, process, and types of listening. Most important, you have studied the 18 instructions for being an effective listener. Now it's time to check yourself to make certain you understand these instructions and are ready to practice them. Read the instructions summarized in the box on the following page. If you understand them and can put them into practice, you are on your way to becoming a first-rate listener—the kind speakers like to have in their audiences and the kind people like to be around. What's more, you'll learn a lot.

A good listener is not only popular everywhere, but after a while he knows something.	**INSIGHT**
Wilson Mizner	

Exercise | Check Yourself: Make Certain You Understand These 18 Instructions

1. Think of listening as a complex process that takes work and discipline.
2. Make long-term, mid-term, and short-term preparations for effective listening.
3. Adjust to the communication situation.
4. Focus on ideas or key points rather than just the facts.
5. Capitalize on the speed differential—the difference between speaking and reading rates.
6. Relate what the speaker is saying to what you already know.
7. Get the right attitude—you must want to listen.
8. Delay judgment.
9. Examine your biases so that they do not unduly affect your listening.
10. Don't tune out dry subjects.
11. Accept your responsibility as listener for understanding what is said.
12. Encourage others when they are speaking.
13. Establish eye contact with the speaker.
14. Be an effective note taker.
15. Be a physically involved listener.
16. Avoid negative mannerisms.
17. Exercise and stretch your listening muscles.
18. Follow the Golden Rule: Listen to others as you would have them listen to you.

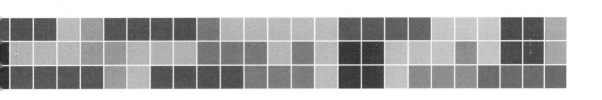

Index